D1398030

Coaching Set Plays

By
Tony Waiters

World of Soccer Ltd.
Vancouver, B.C. • Ferndale, WA

The Coaching Series

Coaching 6, 7 & 8 Year Olds
Coaching 9, 10 & 11 Year Olds
Coaching the Team
Coaching the Player
Coaching the Goalkeeper
Coaching Set Plays

Other Coaching Materials

Teaching Offside
Zonal Defending
Ace Coaching Cards

Children's Activity Books

Soccer is Fun 1, 2 & 3
Hotshots 1, 2 & 3

Canadian Cataloguing In Publication Data
Waiters, Tony
        Coaching set plays : incorporating the 12 key principles for set play success
(Coaching series)
ISBN 1-896466-15-X
        1. Soccer--Coaching. I. Title. II. Series
GV943.8.W342 1999   796.334'2   C99-900827-7

Copyright ©1999 Tony Waiters World of Soccer

First published July 1st, 1999 by WORLD OF SOCCER
5880 Falcon Road, West Vancouver, British Columbia
(800) 762-2378

Email: info@worldofsoccer.com
URL: www.worldofsoccer.com

CREDITS:
Editor: Bob Dunn, Dunn Communications Ltd.
Graphics: James McLeod, 442 Communications
Layout and Design: Lincoln Dunn, Idesign Graphics

Manufactured by Hemlock Printers Ltd., Vancouver, Canada

Acknowledgements

James MacLeod
Bob Dunn
Lincoln Dunn
Anne Waiters
Chuck Dehnert

To my first "coach," Big Brother Mick.

Table of Contents

Anecdotes
Table of Contents

Foreword

Set Plays are detail stuff, but so important. You may want to take it a little at a time. We recommend that you start by reading the Introduction, but where you go from there is your choice.

You may want to look at Chapter 9: "How to Teach and Coach Set Plays" to see what the methodology possibilities are. Or perhaps you are having problems defending at Corners. Then you should go to Chapters 2 and 3.

Our recommendation is that even if your team is not defending well at Corners, it will be a good idea to read the Attacking Corners chapter first. We need to be inside the "minds" of the opponents to beat them at their own game.

We also recommend you take a careful look at the legend below to make sure you understand how the illustrations are being presented. There is an explanation of the rationale we've employed with the graphics, to be as precise as possible.

Certain terminology used in this book might throw you. Have a look at page 10 and the Glossary of Terms on page 93.

The video that partners the book will give real, live examples of Set Plays in action, with animated graphics to show the detailed progression of a Set Play. Both the book and the video can stand on their own, but together they'll be even more powerful.

For instance, there is much more detail in the book than we can cover in the video. On the other hand "a picture is worth a thousand words" and a "live" picture is even better.

If your season is still a long way off, then go through the book at your leisure, from cover to cover.

Tony Waiters

LEGEND

Defending Player

Attacking Player

Path of Ball

Path of Player

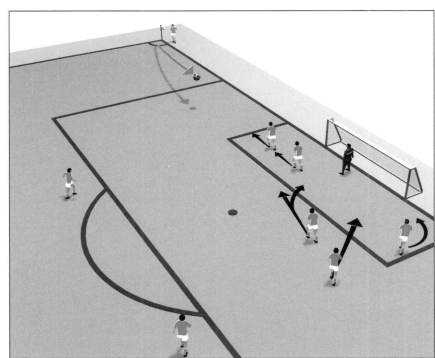

Introduction to Set Plays

The Difference Between Winning and Losing

Statistics can be dangerous in sport. In fact, the expression is: "Statistics are for the losers!" How many losing coaches, stat sheet in hand, have been caught in the statistical web as they explain to the media — and anyone else who cares to listen — why they should have won but didn't?

So it may well be that statistics are for losers. But in soccer, the stats on Set Plays…are for winners! Make no mistake about it!

While statistics around the soccer world vary from year to year, from competition to competition, from age-group to age-group, they still produce an amazing and indisputable fact. The fact is a significant percentage of all goals are a direct or indirect result of Set Plays.

In some competitions, and in some eras, it has been calculated that as many as 60% of all goals have been scored from Set Plays …in others, as low as 25%. Never have I seen it lower than 25%. So let's take the low figure — 25% — one of every four goals!

Do you, as a coach, spend 25% or more of your tactical and team preparation time working on Set Plays?

I'm not a statistician, but I know the answer. I'd bet my last dollar that at least 95% of soccer coaches around the world spend much less than 25% of their team coaching time working on Set Plays.

At your peril!

In a 20-game season, what if you could guarantee scoring five more goals and conceding five less — a 10-goal spread? The difference between a championship season and mediocrity…or a good, fun season rather than a miserable one?

Good and Bad Experiences

This book is the product of 30 years of joyful — and painful! — experiences, both as a player and a coach. The truth is my coaching experiences were much happier with regard to Set Plays because of lessons learned as a player and then quickly learned as a rookie coach.

This book is for real. There will be no BS. The principles and methods outlined in the following pages really WORK! They have been proven over years of successful application.

I recommend you don't try to read this manual all at once — unless the season is coming up soon! Read the early pages to give an overview introduction and the first chapter dealing with the "Principles of Set Plays" and then take your time to digest the information.

Once you've completed the book, use it for reference purposes to refresh your ideas and to stimulate adjustments to your coaching methodology and specific team tactics.

What Are Set Plays?

Set Plays are sometimes referred to as "re-starts" or "dead-ball situations." When a game begins or is or re-started after the ball goes out of play, or after a goal is scored, or the game is stopped for an infringement or injury, the game must start in a given way. So re-starts include Goal Kicks, Throw-ins, Kick-offs, Corner Kicks, direct or indirect Free Kicks, Penalty Kicks and Dropped Balls.

All are Set Plays.

The term Set Play is most appropriate because we are not just "re-starting" the game. As coaches and as a team, we are seeking to gain an attacking advantage from the "opportunity" given by a re-start.

Most Set Play goals come from Penalty Shots, Free Kicks, Throw-ins and Corner Kicks. So that's where we'll concentrate our efforts in this book. However, some goals come as a direct result of Goal Kicks and Kick-offs — even "dropped balls" — so these Set Plays must not be ignored.

For instance, goals are sometimes conceded from mis-directed or mis-kicked Goal Kicks — frequently among young players — and goals are scored indirectly from Goal Kicks — particularly at the higher levels of the game. So this less-spectacular Set Play re-start must not be neglected.

The areas for concentration from a team perspective should be Free Kicks, Corner Kicks and Throw-ins, as these occur frequently — with many occurring in the final third of the field, where a goal can be scored with one or two passes or shots.

Penalties give a certain goal! Or do they? Frequently, they turn the game around. So they must be practiced both from an attacking and defending perspective. And in terms of conceding Penalties, the golden rule is...don't! It can cost a goal, a player and the game!

Discipline and discretion in and around the Penalty Box is critical. In tournament play, Penalties are often tie-breakers. So you must have quality penalty kickers in numbers — not just one or two specialists.

Set Play opportunities are associated, in the main, with competitive 11-vs-11 soccer, but you will see in the appendix, we have a section on the Ages of Set Plays, as young children need to be taught how to start and re-start the game. For instance, the Throw-in is a difficult technique for beginners, as is the Goal Kick, and children need help in overcoming this difficulty.

Terminology – "Near" and "Far"

Voltaire, the great French philosopher, once said: "To converse with me first you must define your terms."

At the back of the book is a short Glossary of Terms highlighting some of the words that may need some definition. For instance, two expressions commonly used in soccer can be confusing to someone who has not been exposed to them — "Near Post" and "Far Post."

For instance, "Take the Near Post" doesn't usually mean a player literally stands at or on the Near Post. It normally means covering the area out and in front of the Near Post.

You could "Take the Far Post!" and still be 20 yards or more from the goal because of the protection afforded by the offside rule.

Or playing "A ball to the Near Post" from a Free Kick out on the wings and 40 yards from goal might be into an area 16-18 yards from the actual Near Post — just behind the "line of defense" that the opposition has set up 20 yards from the goal.

So be careful when interpreting "Near" and "Far" or "Near Post" and "Far Post." Generally speaking "Near" and "Far" refers to areas — not to actual goal posts.

Where the "post" is physically marked, such as at a defending corner, we will specify more clearly that it involves the marking of the post.

PREVENTION IS BETTER THAN A CURE

If, as the statistics tell us, a significant number of goals are scored from Set Plays, it stands to reason that you should not gratuitously give them away — particularly in dangerous situations. How many Penalties have been the result of reckless challenges where the attacking player was nowhere near close to scoring? Too many! A Penalty Kick is not a certain goal, but it's as close as it comes.

By the same rule, stupid Free Kicks and unnecessary Corner Kicks conceded are not the hallmarks of good players and good teams. The difficulty is being an aggressive defender while remaining cool and challenging. But that's what good defenders are. Aggressive, but in control. Reckless, non-calculating defenders are a liability. Death to all coaches!

The 12 Principles for Set Plays Success

The great advantage of Set Plays, particularly from the attacking team's perspective, is that you can arrange your players in the most effective positions. The timing in taking the Set Play is in your hands, or rather, your feet — unless it is a Throw-in. Then it's in the attacking team's hands (or feet)! This is becoming complicated! Let's move on!

For the attacking team, while you control the timing, quick Free Kicks, Corners and Throw-ins can catch the opposition off guard. On the other hand, with nothing better on the horizon, a "Set" Play allows you to arrange — or set up — your players exactly where they are likely to be the most effective. (A note of caution: If you take too much time getting set up, you may alienate the referee and could be penalized for "time-wasting.")

Although the defending team's players don't have the privilege of deciding when the Set Play is to take place, they usually have some time to arrange themselves in their best defending positions.

For years, "professional ploys" have been used by defenders to delay the taking of Free Kicks, Corners and Throw-ins, but today's referees are much more aware of these "tricks." Good coaches avoid these questionable tactics — they only antagonize the referee anyway. Persist, and you may suffer then…or later!

If defending players are alert and aware, and glancing at the referee and the player(s) on the ball, they can determine just how much time they have, and try to put their players in their best positions.

Putting "square pegs in round holes" for Set Plays is costly. This is something the coach must work out with the players — without being too democratic. From personal experience, I know all players have a favorite Free Kick (and Corner Kick) on which they are usually at the center! The coach must eventually determine who does what, when and where, and get the players to "buy in" to that thinking.

The part of the field in which the re-start takes place determines what can and can't be done.

For instance, attacking Free Kicks from the back third of the field are taken with different considerations than a Free Kick in the Front Third. While the objective remains the same — score a goal — it usually takes more than one or two kicks from the Back Third. But in the final third of the field, two kicks — often one — may well produce the shot on goal and score.

Precautionary measures are necessary in the Back Third and Middle Third to avoid the risk of giving the ball away in a part of the field where attacking players are suddenly vulnerable to the counter-attack.

12 Principles for

The 12 Key Principles for Set Plays Success are at work on every Set Play, and as a coach you must understand these "principles" — and so must your players. The 12 Key Principles are:

1. ATD   Attention to Detail

Attention to relevant detail is the key. That's your job! We know that "paralysis by analysis" sets in if players are subjected to the microscopic detail. The coach offsets potential paralysis by being disciplined enough to work on (a) the detail of the Set Plays, and (b) how to present them to the players in the most time-efficient, non-boring way.

2. TRIPLE A'S   Always Alert & Alive

The ball goes dead! The brain goes dead! It is ever thus in soccer. Therefore, it's critical — both from an attacking and defensive perspective — that players are indoctrinated with the requirements to be totally aware and alert for things that happen quickly: a chance lost or a mistake made.

3. SQUARE PEGS   & Round Holes

Square Pegs in Round Holes makes no sense in Set Plays. Most dead-ball situations present an opportunity to put your players in their most effective attacking positions before play resumes. Similarly in defense, although the opposition has the ball and therefore the initiative, and the referee controls the re-start of the game, there is a way of creating time to place your players before that happens.

4. KISS   Keep It Simple, Stupid!

On paper, planning the seven-pass move at the attacking Free Kick looked good, but it never got beyond the second pass! Ron Moran, a former coaching colleague of mine, once joked they had spoiled the game by introducing opponents! Until then it was easy. The simpler the move with the least number of passes and players in the actual execution, the greater the chance of success.

5. FADS   Fakes And Distractions

Diversionary tactics that are not a direct part of the execution of the Free Kicks, Corners and Throw-ins can be effective in distracting opponents and pulling them into false positions. The FADS needs to be orchestrated by the coach to produce maximum effectiveness. Timing will be key.

6. GIFTS   Take What You're Given

Players should always be on the alert for "gifted situations" presented by the opposition and act accordingly. Why complicate the play if the opposition has marked badly and set up a non-covering wall? Take what you're given and score that goal. When there are no gifts, the rehearsed Set Play… comes into play!

Set Plays Success

7. SPACEMEN   Spaces & Bases

This applies both in attacking and defending. No matter what your main system of play is — zonal marking or man-marking — certain spaces and bases must be covered to eliminate the unknown, the unexpected and the "lucky break." On a Corner Kick, no matter what the opponents do, the area in and around the six-yard box must rate prime consideration. Do you put a defender(s) marking the post(s) to defend a Corner Kick? Spaces, and the starting bases that you attack the balls into the spaces from, are the call of the coach and the team. Similarly, from an attacking perspective, putting the ball and attacking players into certain spaces increases the chances of scoring — particularly if a telling ball arrives in the space being attacked (see the "Black Hole," Chapter 2).

8. INSURANCE   Double Cover

Everything doesn't go by the plan. The trick is not to be punished by a mistake. Double cover is implied in "Spaces & Bases" but teams attacking on Set Plays must also ensure that a counter-attack from a failed Set Play has little chance of success. They do this by creating a "ring of confidence" outside the attacking penalty area and by good marking at the half-way line.

9. BALANCE   Team Shape

Bringing players out of their regular positions into the most effective Set Play positions can unbalance the team if the ball stays in play. There may be no time to allow certain players to return to their normal positions. If you're successful, it gives plenty of time as you get ready for the kick-off after the goal! Coaches need to have a way of dealing with the situation by maintaining team balance, or team shape, until a game stoppage allows all players to return to their regular positions.

10. EXO   Execution

This is the principal key principle. There is no point in bringing your 6'4" center back up for a corner and then kicking the ball out of play. Or worse, pulling the ball back too far and not only eliminating your 6'4" center-back, but putting the opposition on a counter attack (minus your center back!). The execution must be practiced to near-perfection. The question that you as the coach must continually ask is: "Have I got the right people for the job in executing this particular Set Play?"

11. REBOUNDS   Seconds

Joe Fagan, the former manager/coach of Liverpool Football Club, used to say "All forwards should be optimists; all defenders should be pessimists." In other words, every player should be expecting the unexpected and be ready to react. If attackers are optimists, "lucky goals" will be scored. The pessimistic defender covering the goalkeeper who goes out to catch a high corner, on the other hand, is "lucky" to stop a goal-bound shot after the keeper missed the ball. Luck is for the lottery player, not the soccer player! Rebounds are always likely to happen on Set Plays — particularly at Free Kicks and Corners.

12. RECOVERY   Redemption

"Recovery" is the requirement of every player, to redeem the situation when possession has been lost at a Set Play. It has to be an instilled quality in all players if the team is to succeed.

If you follow these 12 principles as a coach, and if your players understand the requirements of the principles of Set Plays, you are on your way to scoring goals in re-start situations. At the same time, you'll make it much more difficult for the opposition to score.

Soccer is not a game of luck. It is a game of "percentages." The more times you do the right thing, the greater the chance there is of scoring. The better organized you are defending at re-starts and the more skilled the team's response is once the Set Play is under way, the less goals you allow. Nothing is perfect. The ones nearest to perfection are the winners.

THIRDS OF THE FIELD

The area of the field from where a Set Play takes place determines the attitude and overall philosophy both in attacking and defending. This is particularly true on Free Kicks and Throw-ins. For the purpose of this manual, we're going to revise the terminology of the thirds to avoid confusion.

So we will talk about the Back (or bottom) Third, the Middle Third and the Front (or top) Third.

The reason for this is that we'll both attack and defend when the ball is in the Front Third — depending which team is in possession. If we talk about defending in the attacking third, it's almost an contradiction. So we have simplified the terminology.

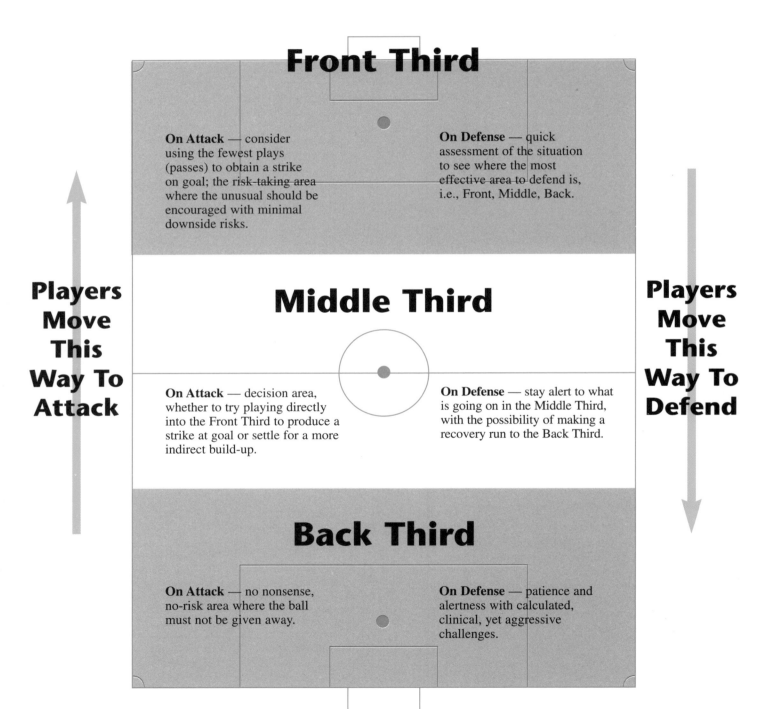

Front Third

On Attack — consider using the fewest plays (passes) to obtain a strike on goal; the risk-taking area where the unusual should be encouraged with minimal downside risks.

On Defense — quick assessment of the situation to see where the most effective area to defend is, i.e., Front, Middle, Back.

Middle Third

On Attack — decision area, whether to try playing directly into the Front Third to produce a strike at goal or settle for a more indirect build-up.

On Defense — stay alert to what is going on in the Middle Third, with the possibility of making a recovery run to the Back Third.

Players Move This Way To Attack

Players Move This Way To Defend

Back Third

On Attack — no nonsense, no-risk area where the ball must not be given away.

On Defense — patience and alertness with calculated, clinical, yet aggressive challenges.

Attacking Corners

In recent years, Corner Kicks have superseded Free Kicks in goals scored from Set Plays. Overall, Penalty Kicks are #1 in goals from re-starts at most levels of competition. We'll come to them in Chapter 7.

The fact is your team attacks and defends many, many more Corners than Penalties. And, generally speaking, there are more Corner Kicks in a game than Free Kicks from dangerous positions in and around the penalty area.

Corner Kicks are gladly conceded by a goalkeeper diving desperately across the goal to stop a goal-bound shot. And defenders often concede Corners in a foot race by kicking the ball out of danger.

The fact that Corner Kicks are being played into the scoring zone from lateral positions makes defending the ball less predictable than shots and service coming in from more central positions. It's one reason so many goalkeepers have problems dealing with crosses.

Don't fall into the trap of the 7 P's of soccer coaching — Poor Planning and Preparation Produce Particularly Poor Performance. Corner Kicks and Set Plays must be practiced.

There are many different types of Corner Kicks. I'm going to deal with the four most successful ones — both from attacking and defending perspectives:

1. The Near Post Corner

2. The Far Post Corner

3. The Short Corner

4. The Pull Back

Before going into the detail, let me introduce you on the next page to the "Black Hole."

Attacking Player

Defending Player

Path of Ball

Path of Player

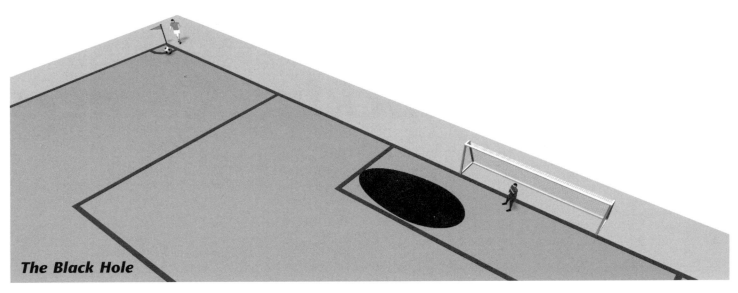

The Black Hole

Any well-hit, well-flighted, usually inswinging ball that arrives head-high in the black area gives great potential for a goal. In fact, an overhit inswinging ball will likely produce a scoring opportunity in the mid-goal and Far Post areas.

I find it difficult to believe how many teams still ignore the great scoring opportunity created by balls into the "Black Hole" area. How often do you see them ballooning the ball to the Far Post areas, only to see the central defenders time and time again rise to clear the ball with headers?

I'm not saying outswinging Far Post balls are a waste of time. Of course, they're not.

What I am saying is that in most competitions, more goals are scored from balls played initially to the Near Post "Black Hole" area than those played to the Far Post area. Facts don't lie.

The "perfect" ball is a well-flighted inswinger arriving head-high into the eye of the "Black Hole" — just too far forward for the keeper to take comfortably. (See illustration bottom right)

THE NEAR POST (INSWINGING OR INSWINGER) CORNER

Most "Near Post" Corners are inswingers — with the left foot from the right side and with the right foot from the left side. However, there are some very skillful kickers who can swerve an inswinging ball or straight ball with the right foot from the right side (or the left foot from the left side). Teams containing only "mere mortals" have to settle for right from left and vice-versa and make the necessary organizational arrangements.

Defending teams should consider putting a defender 10 yards from the Corner Kick to make the kicking job more difficult, but the 10-yard rule means it's not that much of a deterrent. That defender may be more useful in another critical defending area. However, the player stationed near the corner flag is discouraging the short corner and needs only one more teammate to neutralize a 2-vs-1.

Nevertheless, in practice, it's worthwhile practicing the kick with and without a 10-yard marker.

It really doesn't matter what the opposition does with regard to its defensive organization if the "execution" of the planned Corner Kick is good. So let's look at the set-up, the positions and the actions that are required.

It's worth considering having two attacking players out at the Corner Kick, to give the alternative of a short corner, and the option of an inswinger or an outswinger. However, you may not want to risk getting too many players on the "wrong side of the ball" if there is a clearance and counter attack. Two attackers at the corner pull at least one — usually two — defenders out of the penalty area. This is a judgment call that has to be made by the coach.

First of all, let's take the situation we see in the illustration on the next page and look at the roles and expectations of each player.

Coaches! Please understand this is not the one and only way this play can be executed. You may have players moving from blindside positions into the areas where I have players standing. The "principles" are key here and I have added the "job descriptions" of each player to clearly delineate the job performance that's expected.

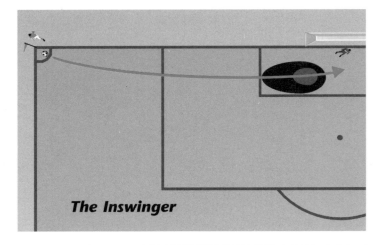

The Inswinger

Player 1

The Corner Kicker. This player is guaranteed to be part of the execution. No one else is. Almost everything depends on the quality of the actual kick (see the "How To Teach and Coach Set Plays," Chapter 9, including the identification and selection process).

Aim the ball at where **Player 3** is standing — arriving at a height of 7 feet to 7 1/2 feet. The over-hit ball and the slightly under-hit ball still works for us.

There are two types of kicks that are particularly effective:

a. A fairly fast ball that does not deviate too much in its trajectory and is extremely difficult for the defenders to judge.

b. A slower, higher ball (not too high or it's easier for the keeper) that arrives from a slightly higher trajectory, and is more difficult for the defenders to time their jumps and runs. The defenders could end up doing the jobs of Player 2 or Player 3.

Player 2

Player 2 is positioned towards the front of the "Black Hole" to make the most of a slightly under-hit ball. It matters not if **Player 2** is marked front and back, which may well be the case, and the player does not need to get involved with the opposition and end up in a pushing and shoving match. **Player 2** holds position until the ball is played. **Player 2** does not try to get any ball he or she needs to go backwards to play. **Player 3** looks after that. Instead, **Player 2** flicks the ball on from the assigned position, or move forwards three or four yards to make a deflection contact with the badly under-hit ball.

The flick-on trajectory and direction is critical. It's just enough to eliminate the defenders immediately behind.

See the illustration on the next page.

Player 2's trajectory is slightly higher than that of **Player 3's.**

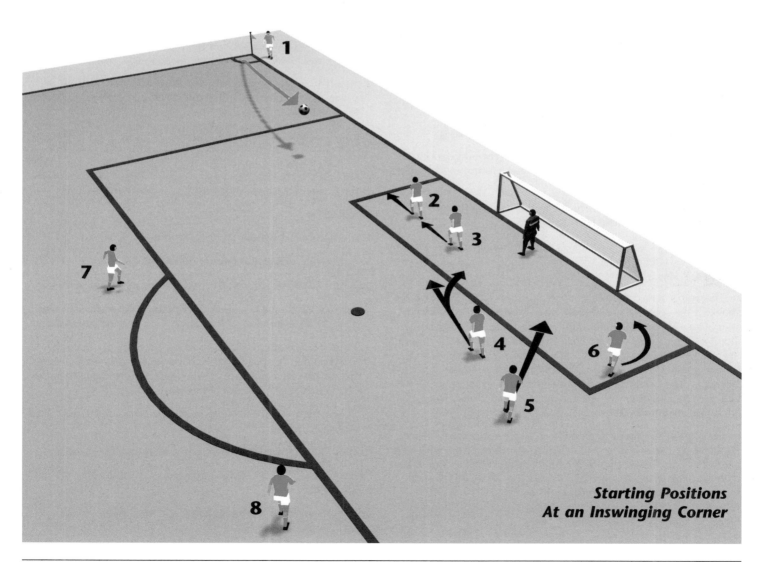

Starting Positions
At an Inswinging Corner

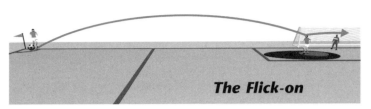

The Flick-on

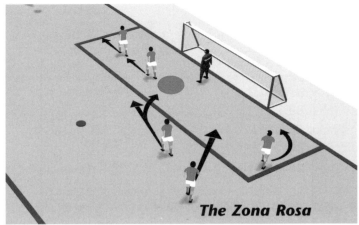

The Zona Rosa

Ideally, with both flick-ons, the actual direction of the ball is unchanged. This makes it much easier for the players attacking the spaces to "read" and anticipate while leaving the defenders uncertain as to what might happen. This depends on the quality of **Player 1's** kick, as the ball may need to be re-directed if it's a little off-course.

If the inswinging cross is really badly under-hit, **Player 2** has to make the most of it and move out towards the ball before a defender does, and glide it on with the head or foot, or even consider a right-footed knock back at 90 degrees, to Player 7.

Player 3

Player 3 is the "Target Man" and takes up a position approximately 3 to 4 yards out from the Near Post, about two feet inside the line of the post in the "eye" of the Black Hole. Once again, in spite of the attention **Player 3** may receive from the opposition, the player endeavors not to become involved and just remain in position as the target for **Player 1. Player 3** assesses the ball coming in and may have to make a short two- or three-yard run to arrive at the ball just in front of the Near Post, where there are three alternatives:

1. A little flick-on for Player 5 or Player 6 to convert.

2. **A glancing header at goal, where a re-directed head ball sliding sideways off the forehead is next to impossible for the goalkeeper to read.**

3. **A full-contact header to the Near Post, powerful and giving the keeper little time to react.**

Alternative #1 is the most likely and #2 is more likely than #3.

Player 4

This is the most difficult and the bravest run of all. **Player 4** is attacking the space just beyond the very back of the "Black Hole" — what we've called the Red Zone, or the Zona Rosa. Generally, this is on the slightly over-hit Near Post ball with **Player 4** making the first contact for a shot — usually a header, and often a diving header at that. Or it's a foot volley directly at goal. It may require a "physical confrontation" to make contact. The "fight" to get to the ball must be fair, otherwise the initiative is surrendered. Faint hearts are not employable in this situation! (Square Pegs).

Player 4 may also be attempting to make contact with the under-hit ball that **Player 2** has flicked-on. Here again, **Player 4** needs to "fight" to be first to the ball. If **Player 3** flicks on from the back half of the Black Hole, **Player 4** is likely eliminated from the play and it's left to **Player 5** or **Player 6** — but not necessarily (Triple A) and (Gifts). Many Corner Kick goals end up being scored in the Red Zone.

Player 5

Player 5 is the Far Post specialist, perhaps a defender who has moved up for the play. This player must be aware of several possibilities and be prepared to react accordingly:

1. **Convert the "flick-on" from Player 2 or Player 3.**

2. **Make the first contact on an over-hit ball missing the Near Post players and arriving at the Far Post.**

3. **React to a mis-judged ball by all players that arrives near the ground and scoots across the six-yard box.**

4. **React to a misplaced, mis-kicked clearance with an unclaimed ball spinning around the Far Post area of the six-yard box.**

Player 6

This is the player looking for the "Garbage Goal." The player is rewarded if the gamble is taken consistently. **Player 6** arrives in the space at the back of the goal as the ball arrives from:

1. **A flick-on.**

2. **A misdirected header for goal by Player 3.**

3. **A mis-shot clearance from a defender.**

4. **A mis-handled attempt to catch the cross by the keeper.**

5. **A ball that eludes everyone as it bends across the six-yard box and destined for a Goal Kick if no one makes contact.**

Player 6 is "loitering" but can't be too far away from the area where the "garbage goal" can be scored. **Player 6,** usually a smaller player, starts from an inconspicuous position beyond the Far Post (see "Loitering With Intent," page 24).

Remember the Square Pegs in Square Holes and Round Pegs in Round Holes?

Player 1 must be able to execute in games as well as practice.

Player 2 must be disciplined and good at the flick-on with the head and feet.

Player 3 must have excellent heading ability and a "magic touch" for the subtle flick-on.

Player 4 must be brave yet skilled, with excellent timing.

Player 5 must be a classic Far Post header of the ball, but aware enough to make the most of what comes into that area.

Player 6 has to be disciplined and optimistic to keep making the runs — and then Mr. Cool to finish off the "Garbage Goal."

The rest of the team needs to be primed ready for action. **Player 7** and **Player 8** are ready to join the action for a partial clearance or a ball that's hooked out, but also give that "ring of confidence" to stop the opposition catching the attacking team on a breakaway in the transition.

Players 9 and **10** (not shown here) mark front and back if the opposition leaves one player up on the halfway line — as many do — or move towards the "Ring of Confidence." **Player 9** or **Player 10** move further forward should the defending team pull all players back to defend the corner.

That's why you may not have the luxury of being able to put two players on the Corner Kick — it may make you shorthanded outside the penalty area or at the half-way line.

FAR POST CORNERS

Far Post Corners work on the same principles of attack as Near Post Corners — except the execution and the spaces are different. Normally the Far Post

corner is taken right-footed from the right and left-footed from the left, but not necessarily so.

An inswung corner to the Far Post can be very effective, particularly if the defending team is not sure what to expect and is geared to defending heavily at the "Black Hole".

There is an advantage in having two players at the Far Post who are both capable of attacking high crosses. This way, the defending team has doubled its problem — where and who to mark, and it increases the opportunity for the attacking team to use fakes, blocks and crossovers to fool the opposition.

For the purpose of this manual, I'm going to concentrate on the outswinging Far Post kick, with two players at the back post (remember not to leave yourself at risk and short of players for the failed corner and quick counter attack…1-vs-1 at the back is quite a gamble — not one I would take!).

Player 1 is the only player in the action who is guaranteed a kick. It needs to be a good one to increase the chances of scoring. If the ball is "floated" too much, it gives the opposition time to adjust and attack the cross. Accuracy is an important factor. The "worst ball" is the one played too far out (between the penalty spot and the top of the box and beyond) as it can put the defending team quickly into an attacking mode with too many "now defending" players caught on the wrong side of the ball.

Player 2 is positioned in the Near Post area but two or three yards further out than the inswinging corner to accommodate the out-swinger. This player is there to make contact with the mis-hit or under-hit corner and make the most of what comes in (see role of **Player 2** at the inswinging corner Page 17).

Attacking Roles and Positions at an Outswinging Corner

For the Far Post ball, **Player 2** spins out and round, looking to connect for a "garbage goal" on a ball that misses everyone on the Far Post header/shot and is going wide of the opposite post.

Player 3 attacks the space behind **Player 2** for the slightly under-hit cross. If nothing else the run helps clear the space for **Player 4** and **Player 5** in the Far Post area. If **Player 3** does not get the direct header, he or she spins out and repositions for the header back across the goal but further out than **Player 2**. **Player 3** needs to read the situation and respond accordingly.

Player 4 and **Player 5** are attacking in the Far Post areas in a conventional manner. However, it may worth working on some staggered and blocking runs to confuse the marking defenders — particularly if the defending team is man-marking. But remember the KISS principle as you don't want to fake yourself out of making a strong, well-timed attacking run. On an under-hit ball, **Players 4** and **5** look for the flicked-on ball from **Player 2** or **Player 3** at the Far Post.

Player 6 looks for the over-hit Far Post ball to play as he or she "sees" it. The priority option is to play the ball back across the six-yard box. Player 6 must have good penalty area "instincts" and could find the time to end in the "garbage collector's" area.

Players 7 and **8** are providing the "ring of confidence" and containment outside the area.

Players 9 and **10** (not shown) mark front and back of any lone opponent left up field at the halfway line as an outlet for the clearance and should not be allowed one inch of space ("live inside their shorts"). If an opponent is not left up field, then either **Player 10** or **Player 9** can move and join the "ring of confidence."

SHORT CORNERS

One simple variation of the Inswinging Corner is shown in the illustration below where **Player 1** uses a "short corner" technique to produce a more effective angle for the cross. **Player 1** plays the ball to **Player 2**, who is three yards away. **Player 2** stops the ball and moves back a pace to allow **Player 1** to inswing the ball from a more favorable angle than a direct Corner Kick.

Stopping the ball with the sole of the foot recreates a "dead-ball" situation for the kicker and helps produce greater accuracy. The

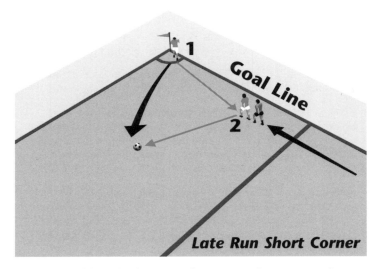

Late Run Short Corner

opposition will send at least one player — maybe two — to the 10-yard position so time and space are factors in the execution. Be aware that you're also running short of "bodies" in attacking tactics, so some adjustment to the organization of the previous inswinging corner is necessary — because two players are committed at the corner flag, which gives you one player less in other areas.

Alternatively, **Player 2** can move out of the Penalty Box and so create more space for the kicker, but this time having to control a moving pass (see illustration above).

Short Corners, for players young and old, give a wonderful opportunity of gaining clear possession in a very telling area of the Final Third. In addition to the Short Corner/Inswinging Corner combination, the "short corner" gives two other advantages:

1. **It improves the angle for the balls played in to the Far Post (and Near Post).**

2. **It encourages the opposition to send out two players from the ultimate scoring zone, therefore leaving them less capable of marking spaces and players in front of goal.**

Let us look at the two other methods for Short Corners with 2-vs-1 situations:

In the illustration below, the defender may discourage **Player 2** from going down the goal line, but by doing so opens

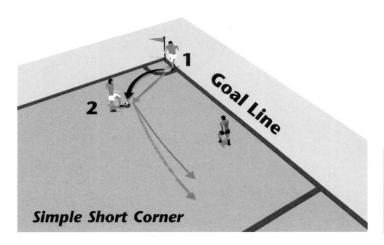

Simple Short Corner

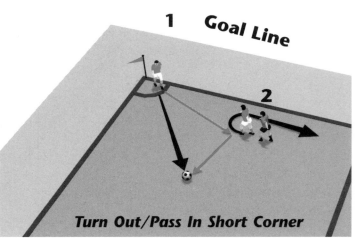

Turn Out/Pass In Short Corner

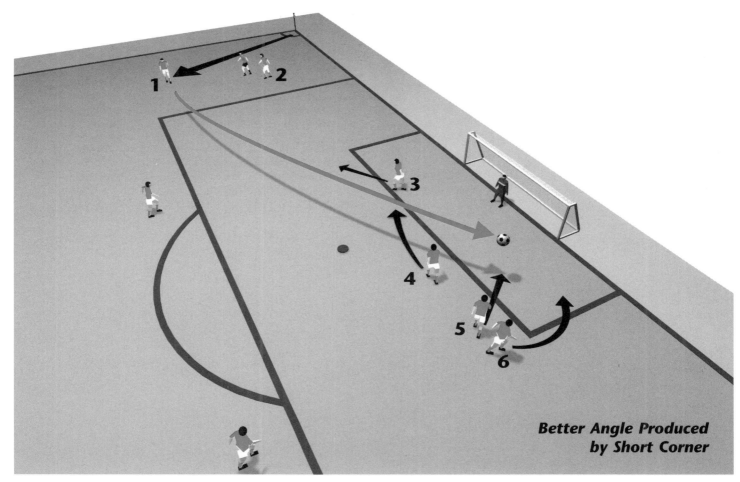

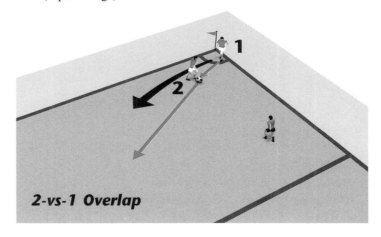

**Better Angle Produced
by Short Corner**

up the space for **Player 1** to take a pass from **Player 2** (difficult for the defender in a 2-vs-1 to prevent both). **Player 1's** angle is now good for at least four options — Near Post, Far Post, dribble in, or pass to a player on top of the box.

As we see in the illustration above, with **Player 1** in position to play the ball in, the defenders have a dilemma. Do they hold their defending positions in the six-yard box? Or do they move up five or six yards to take advantage of the offside? Remember: **Player 1** has limited time in which to decide which action to take because a defender will move quickly towards **Player 1** to close him or her down.

Player 2 and **Player 3** need to be aware of offside and be prepared to move out quickly.

Player 4 needs to flatten his run — as opposed to the conventional Near Post corner — to attack the "Black Hole" space.

The best ball by **Player 1** may be the one shown being attacked by **Player 5**. The goalkeeper can't do much about it — unless it is a poorly hit "floating" ball and is eliminating the defenders, who must be prepared to defend the "Black Hole" on the initial set-up.

While **Player 6's** role could be scoring a "garbage goal," it's most likely to be more effective to play a header back across the goal because of the acute angle. **Player 6's** run needs almost-perfect timing in reading the ball without being caught offside.

Arriving a bit too late is not a big deal. It gives the ball back to the opposition for a Goal Kick with time to re-organize and defend. **Player 6** must also be aware that he/she may be dealing with the over-hit in-swinging cross, or a flick-on from the Near Post area. Great area for "Loitering with Intent" (see page 24).

A similar situation can occur from a simple overlap run at a 2-vs-1 corner. **Player 2,** after receiving the ball, plays it to **Player 1,** who has made the overlap run. Naturally **Player 2** evaluates the situation to see if anything is better than what Player 1 offers.

It goes without saying that **Player 1** should have a good right foot (Square Pegs).

2-vs-1 Overlap

THE PULL BACK

As a defense retreats and becomes concentrated in the most dangerous areas (why wouldn't it?), the opportunity for a late run from the back for a right-sided or left-sided defender presents itself.

As everyone pulls in for the anticipated corner into the danger area, a ball is played back into the area shown below. As the defending team adjusts by pushing up, a real opportunity is created in the space immediately behind.

Near Post, Far Post and "garbage runs" can all be effective here. There is one major problem...and it must be addressed and practiced.

When the ball is played back to the incoming rear defender, there must be enough time and — therefore — space for the

defender to take two touches of the ball: the first to control, the second to set up the next action.

Playing a first-time ball in is the ideal. If it's accurate, that's the best of all worlds because it catches the opposition wrong-footed. The reality is very few players have the composure and ability to play an accurate first-time cross. Bumpy soccer fields further compound this problem. The space and time to play a set-up touch and then cross is essential.

The Pull Back might seem to be an attractive alternative, but frankly using the KISS principle, there are likely to be many more failures than successes. As well, to keep it 2-vs-1 at the halfway line, a player from the "ring of confidence" should move back to the halfway line (see illustration below).

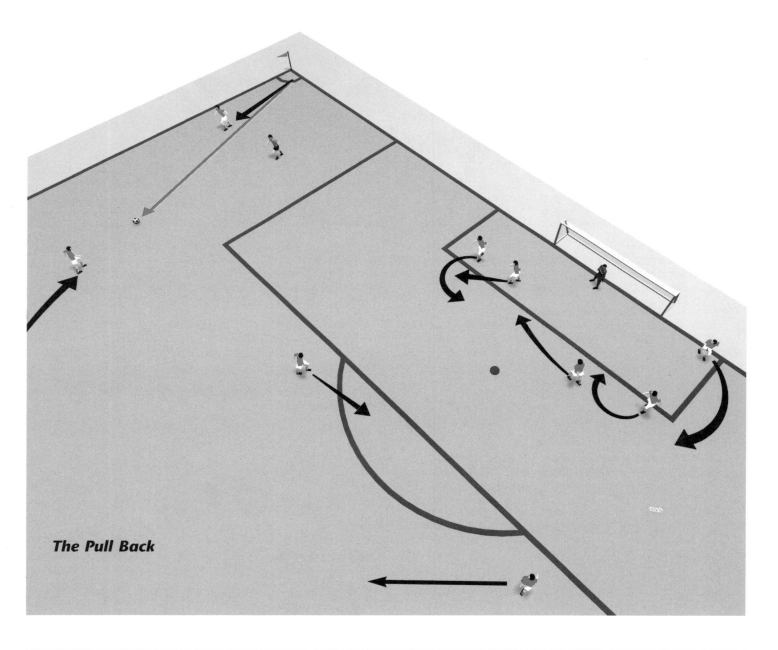

The Pull Back

CONCLUSION

There are many variations of Corner Kicks and we have dealt with some of them in relation to the four most often used.

This illustration below shows how an attacking team can organize itself to offer all four varieties of the options covered at any one corner. The deployment of two attacking players at the corner disallows all "Bases and Spaces" to be covered, but that also applies to the defending team.

These four corners are not the only ones, and variations of them should be considered...such as an Inswinger to the Far Post area.

In soccer, you're always looking to increase the chances of success and reduce the chances of failure. Without being negative, the "re-organization," "reaction" and "recovery" on the transition after an unsuccessful Corner Kick must be planned for and practiced. At certain times in my career, I've been with teams whose opponents were more likely to score when we had won a Corner Kick! Say no more!

Attacking Corners give an incredible opportunity to score a goal. It won't be 50%. It won't be 25%. But if you are organized and execute well, it strikes terror in the hearts of opponents, and produces goals...sooner rather than later!

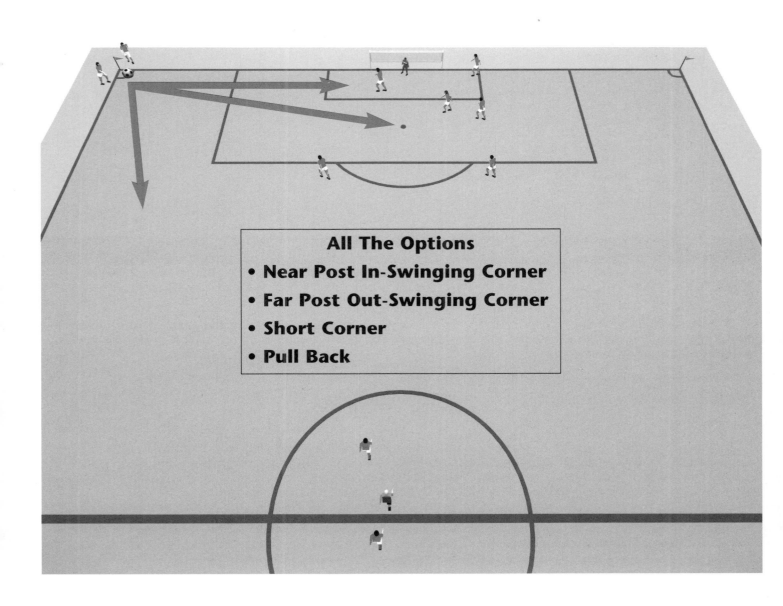

All The Options
- **Near Post In-Swinging Corner**
- **Far Post Out-Swinging Corner**
- **Short Corner**
- **Pull Back**

LOITERING WITH INTENT

If you were accused of "loitering" in Olde England, you could be in serious trouble particularly if you were loitering "with intent." To loiter is to "stand around idly." If you were loitering with intent, you were considered to be "up to no good."

Most times we don't want "loiterers" on the team — except on Set Plays. There is a compelling reason for having a loiterer doing nothing other than hovering or loitering outside the Far Post area — both on wide Free Kicks and Corners Kicks.

How many balls do you see skim across the 6-yard box and go out of play just beyond the Far Post — or stay in play but continue rolling towards the corner flag?

It's a good idea to have one "loiterer with intent" on your team whose only job on Corner Kicks and wide Free Kicks is to sneak into the Far Post area at the appropriate time to pick up that garbage goal. Garbage? It counts just the same as a 30-yard screamer!

The Loiterer

TERRA NOVA!

In 1985, there were three teams remaining in the CONCACAF playdowns for the World Cup the next year in Mexico — Honduras, Costa Rica and Canada. We were playing for just one place, with the host nation already awarded one of CONCACAF's then-two places.

All three countries met in Guatemala City for the draw. In reality, a draw was unnecessary because the three countries all agreed dates and times for the games. The only thing that remained to be announced at the official draw were the venues — the choice of each host nation.

We were last to go. Jim Fleming, President of the Canadian Soccer Association, got to his feet and spoke:

"Canada versus Costa Rico. Toronto!"

"Canada versus Honduras. St. John's!"

"St. John's? St. John's?" repeated the Honduran delegates as they produced a king-sized map of Canada and spread it over their table. They searched the West Coast, the Prairies, then Ontario and Quebec moving towards the Maritimes. Suddenly there was a shout "Terra Nova!" and a finger went up long and high, east and north, to the island and Province of Newfoundland. Their eyes were like organ stops. "Terra Nova! Terra Nova!" They kept repeating.

That was to be the final game in the series. As fate would have it, it was the one that decided who went to Mexico. Two Canadian goals from Inswinging Corners taken by Carl Valentine were the clinchers (see "A funny thing happened on the way to King George V playing field" on page 84).

Defending Corner Kicks

It wouldn't make a lot of sense to have arranged this manual with Defending Corner Kicks preceding Attacking Corners.

The philosophy and the ploy has to be: "If that's what they're going to try to do on Corner Kicks, this is how we are going to stop them!"

No matter what the opposition has up its sleeve, some things are not going to change that much. For instance, a goalkeeper will not stand on the penalty spot to defend a Corner Kick. The keeper will be on or near the goal line somewhere between the Near Post and the Far Post. However, the goalkeeper's position will be adjusted according to the type of Corner likely to be executed — inswinger, outswinger, short corner.

For the benefit of this chapter, we'll deal with defending against the four types of Corner Kicks we highlighted on the attacking chapter, i.e., Inswinger into the Near Post; Outswinger to the Far Post; Short Corners and the Pull Back.

As the defending team, you can't tell the opposition which type of corner you prefer them to take. They make that call. So the defending team must be aware of all contingencies and set up to react accordingly.

If the attacking side sends two players out for a Corner Kick — a left-footer and a right-footer, one on each side of the corner flag — with an outside defender hovering 30 to 40 yards back but inclined towards the flank, the opposition has the options of playing an Inswinger, an Outswinger, a Short Corner or a Pull Back. Or any other trick they may have up their sleeve. That's where we wound up in the last chapter.

As we pointed out in Chapter 2, the "Black Hole" is the area we have to be most concerned about — the No. 1 priority — particularly if the opposition has the ability to deliver telling balls into that area.

Throughout the book, I've used anecdotes to help "color" the serious — dare I say boring! — stuff that Set Plays can be if we're not careful. If you haven't already done so, read "The Inswinging '60s" on page 72 to get an idea of where I'm coming from.

There is another experience I think is worth relating. It happened while I was the youth coach at Liverpool Football Club.

MAN MARKING VS ZONAL DEFENDING

Which is the best way to defend? Man-marking with a sweeper? Or Zonal Marking without a sweeper? The arguments could go on forever! Both methods have produced world champions. As we have quoted Alan Brown, the old Burnley, Sunderland and Sheffield Wednesday manager/coach elsewhere in the manual: "There are many ways up Everest!"

The problem on Corner Kicks, however, can be compounded with a man-marking system if the attacking team overloads the six-yard box. There is too much traffic and confusion for both the keeper and the defenders to handle.

In the '70s, at Liverpool Football Club, our youth players were having problems defending Corner Kicks. We decided to switch to a zonal defending system.

The young players were not comfortable with the change. So co-coach Ronnie Moran suggested a "challenge." It was this. I went in goal (I was only 31 then!). Ron marked the Near Post area. Big Davie Rylands, our 17-year-old dominant central defender, took the Far Post area. We then played against the rest of the players, a fully loaded attack, but with the condition the ball had to be inswung or outswung into the six-yard box, or between the six-yard box and the penalty spot.

They had 25 Corner Kicks and never took a shot at goal. And it wasn't through any heroics by me. Between Dave and Ron, they were first to just about every ball. You see, the job was simple for them and there was no danger of duplication of roles. The "job descriptions" were clear and we all did our jobs.

After that, the defensive problems on Corner Kicks diminished!

It's not for me to say which system of defending you should employ. There is no one best system. That's up to you. However, the illustration below highlights the primary areas that need to be defended on Inswinging and Outswinging Corners.

Area 1 — looked after by the goalkeeper and the post markers.

Area 2 — a question of systems to be employed; in a Zonal Marking system, on an Inswinging Corner, two players are needed to cover the space.

Area 3 — same at the Far Post as one player can't cover both the front of the area and the back.

Area 4 — a key area, but one player from the proper start position should be able to cover it.

Certain decisions are made by the coach and the coach must get the team to "buy in."

1. Do you mark zonally or man-to-man — or a combination of both?

2. Do you commit one player to go 10 yards from the kicker?

3. Do you put defenders on both posts to cover the goal and the goalkeeper?

4. Do you bring everyone back for Defensive Corners and give yourself no outlet with a long clearance ball?

As the coach, you must answer these questions yourself. But I guess I'll show my hand with the organization on the next page. To cause you to think, have a good look at the way I have deployed the defenders. This is the way I'd have my team defend.

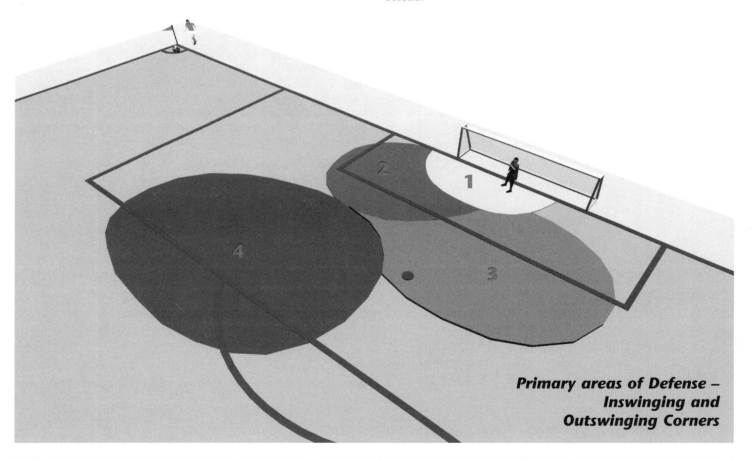

Primary areas of Defense –
Inswinging and
Outswinging Corners

If I was coaching in the pro ranks or at the World Cup level today, I might modify it. But not very much! That's me. Not you. But the "principles" involved and the pinning down of "jobs and duties" is required no matter what the system or strategy.

I'll run through the job lists first, and the possible modifications last.

DEFENDING THE INSWINGER

On the set-up we are showing at the moment, the defending players are positioned to neutralize an Inswinging Corner taken with a right-footed player (below).

The goalkeeper's position is critical. The keeper must get the balls dropping in the back quarter of the Black Hole. With a well-flighted ball coming with some pace into the front half of the Black Hole, even Superman would be in trouble. Our mortal goalkeeper has no chance.

So the keeper's position three yards from the Near Post and one yard off the line is about right. It amazes me how many keepers, even at the highest levels, will take up a central position on an Inswinging Corner — unable to make up the ground to defend the area out from the Near Post.

Player 7 is 10 yards from the ball and doing as much as possible to disturb and distract the kicker (is this a waste of a player?)

Players 2 and **3** are guarding the Near and Far Post. The keeper needs to see the ball, so **Player 2** might be slightly inside

the post — looking at the kicker through the side-netting (do you need a player on the Far Post?).

Should the opposition look to get two players at the corner with the chance of a 2-vs-1, then **Player 2** moves out from the Near Post to help **Player 7**. **Player 3** moves quickly from the Far Post to take the Near Post. The Far Post is sacrificed, but only to a certain extent as **Player 8** moves slightly back to kill more of the space around that area ("Garbage Goals" — see Chapter 2).

Player 4 leans towards the front of the Black Hole and attacks any ball coming in or even short of the Black Hole.

Player 5 attacks the balls in the Black Hole that clear **Player 4** and that the keeper can't reach.

Player 6 attacks the balls clearing **Player 5** and too far out for the keeper, coming into the Red Zone, but because of the more backward position will also have more time to attack high balls in that central area in front of the goal beyond the six-yard box.

Player 8 is the top defensive header of high balls and so becomes the key player in the Far Post area.

Player 9 covers and threatens the area in and around the space shown in the illustration and discourages a low to medium height ball between the six-yard box and the penalty spot, but also reacts quickly if required to move and pressure a Pull Back.

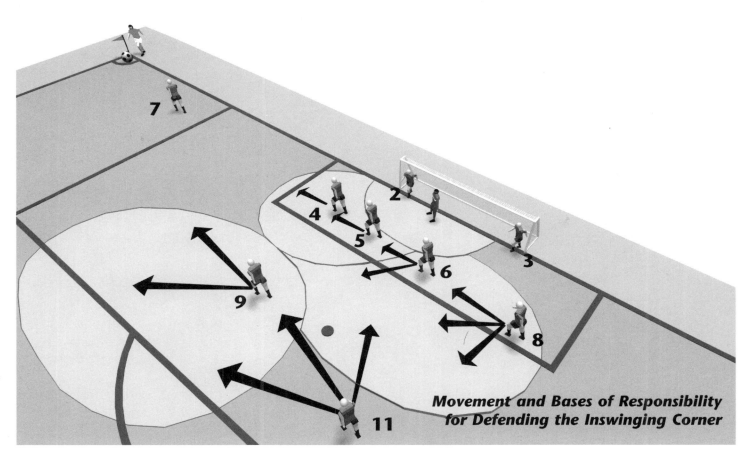

Movement and Bases of Responsibility for Defending the Inswinging Corner

Player 11 is picking up the pieces out towards the top of the Penalty Box and is available on a contingency basis for anything that happens, such as a high ball to the far post area. He may move in more towards **Player 8** to help defend the Far Post Area.

Notice there is no **Player 10** shown. That player is on the halfway line occupying two attackers. As coach, you need to decide whether that player is better employed helping the defense or being an outlet for a clearance as well as occupying two attackers.

I recommend having "speed merchants" in the **Player 9** and **Player 11** positions, so that after a long clearance they could race forward to help get pressure on the ball as quickly as possible.

After a clearance, the back defenders move out as a block — usually quickly — to help the team set up its line of defense as far out as possible and often leaving opposing attackers in offside positions.

DEFENDING THE OUTSWINGER

Remember for both the Inswinger and Outswinger, the positions indicated are the base "starting positions," which may need slight adjustments depending on what is or could be happening.

For instance, if the attacking team pulled four or five players to the "Far Post" and with no apparent threat of a Short Corner or Pull Back, the positions of **Player 7** and **Player 4** are reassessed. **Player 4** could be brought back to help at the Far Post with **Player 7** coming back to fill the position vacated by **Player 4.**

You will notice that in the arrangement for the Outswinger, the basic positions have been modified slightly from the Inswinger, to deal with the different direction and swing of the ball.

Player 7 moves a yard or so towards the goal line.

Players 5 and 6 move out a yard or two.

Player 8 adjusts by three or four yards.

Everyone else adjusts. The **Keeper** takes a more central position and moves out two yards or more off the line. **Player 2** is hands-on-the-post out from the Near Post, and **Player 3** two to three yards out from the Far Post, and so on.

I've always been uncomfortable in pulling everyone back and having no forward outlet player on the halfway line, but the facts of soccer life are we run out of numbers in killing all the dangerous spaces. The opposition has a much better chance of scoring in the next 10 or 20 seconds than we have! As coach, this is your call.

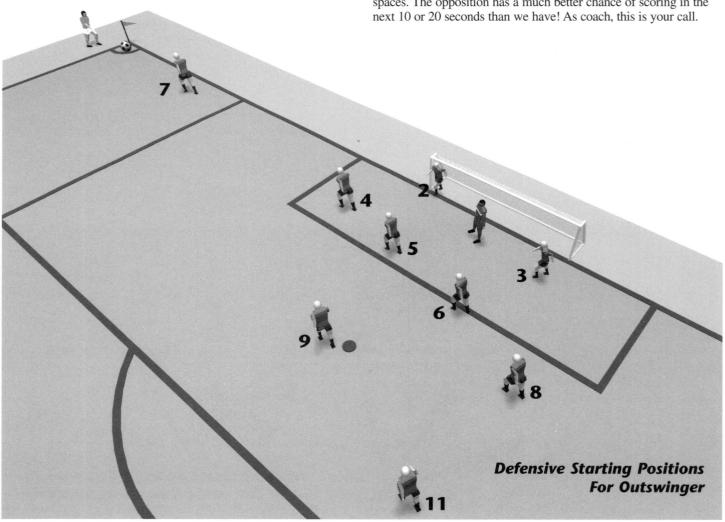

*Defensive Starting Positions
For Outswinger*

You still have to ask yourself the following questions:

Is **Player 7** needed **10** yards out from the corner kicker (it discourages the short corner)?

Can we sacrifice **Player 3** at the Far Post and/or **Player 4** at the front of the Black Hole?

Take one player out of those two areas and you can have a forward outlet on the half-way line. What's more, that forward player keeps at least one (usually two) defenders back.

Notice that I have pulled **Player 9** marginally back towards the Far Post area, but **Player 9** assisted by **Player 7** must be the player(s) to apply pressure on a Pull Back.

Notice I also still have **Player 2** going out to join **Player 7** to make a 2-vs-2 if they put two players at the corner below.

Player 4 could be that player, or **Player 4** could take the post instead of **Player 3.** The problem here is that we are confusing and altering the "Job List" from the Inswinger to the Outswinger. With two attacking players on the Corner Kick, and with the inability to ascertain whether it's going to be an Inswinger, an Outswinger, a Short Corner or a Pull Back, it might be better to work on the KISS principle. So **Player 2** gets the nod (and the order!) to do the Short Corner job.

Player 8 moves back towards the Far Post, to compensate for **Player 3** moving to the Near Post, and **Player 10** drops in to cover area left by **Player 8's** adjustment.

In practice, it's very important to work on what happens after the initial clearance on a Corner Kick. Defending teams must be trained to immediately react (Triple A's) to be first to the ball and not allow "seconds" for the opposition. The first clearance may only be a partial one, perhaps a deflection header out to the flanks. Or it may be a longer clearance up to the half-way line.

Leadership is required from the goalkeeper and back defenders regarding when and how far to move up after a clearance. On a longer clearance, and with or without a player up on the half-way line, the question is: "Who goes to the ball?" Answer: the nearest player! And how quickly can we give that player support? How far and how fast do the back players move out and up?

While the priority, quite clearly, for Defending Corners is to prevent a goal — even a shot — it's a fact that opponents are often caught by a counter-attack. So survival should not be the only thought — think positively, too!

"We will repel this Corner Kick and having done so, we'll get down to the other end and put the pressure on them!"

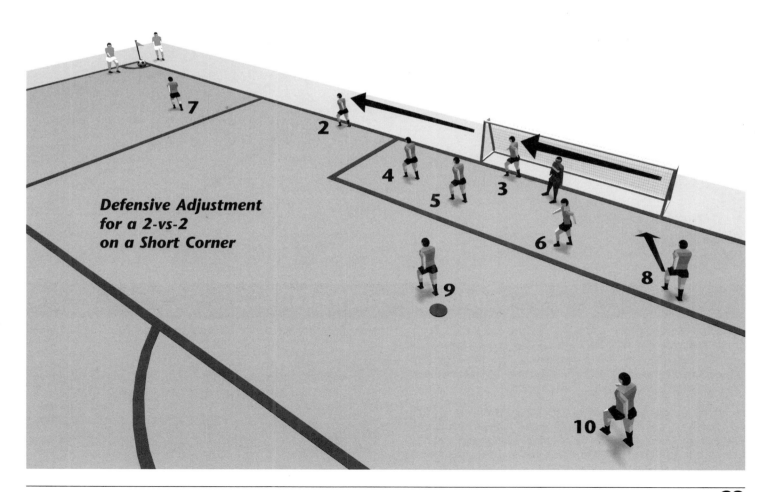

Defensive Adjustment for a 2-vs-2 on a Short Corner

SHORT CORNERS AND PULL BACKS

We've indicated, in discussing Outswinging and Inswinging Corners, how we need to be organized to neutralize, or at least make more difficult, Short Corners and Pull Backs.

On the Short Corner, if a defender is left facing a 2-vs-1, that's nothing new for the defender and is played as such — attempting to delay if help is on the way, or forcing the play into the least dangerous part of the field.

If we get 2-vs-2 on the Short Corner, it's no different than any other 2-vs-2 defensive situation where pressure, cover, patience and discipline will be the order of the day.

On the Pull Back, the nearest player has to get out as quickly as possible to pressure the player with the ball and force a hurried pass or cross. If the pass or cross is prevented, the pressuring player continues to defend as any conventional defender in a 1-vs-1 situation.

ZONAL DEFENDING vs MAN MARKING

In this chapter, I've shown defending Corners from a zonal perspective. That doesn't mean this is way to defend Corners. I've quoted in other books the wise words of Allan Brown, a highly successful coach in the UK in the '60s and '70s who would say: "There are many ways up Everest…!"

If you feel a man-marking system is required, perhaps just for certain players, the system of defending changes but the dangerous spaces do not change. They must be defended resolutely and skillfully.

For instance, in the zonal system I have shown, the Short Corner is negated by getting a second player out to produce a 2-vs-2 — a man-for-man situation.

So no system can be totally zonal or totally man-marking. Dangerous spaces have to be denied to the opposition — one way or another. It is your job as a coach to decide which is to the most effective way to defend — and then follow the "Principles of Set Plays."

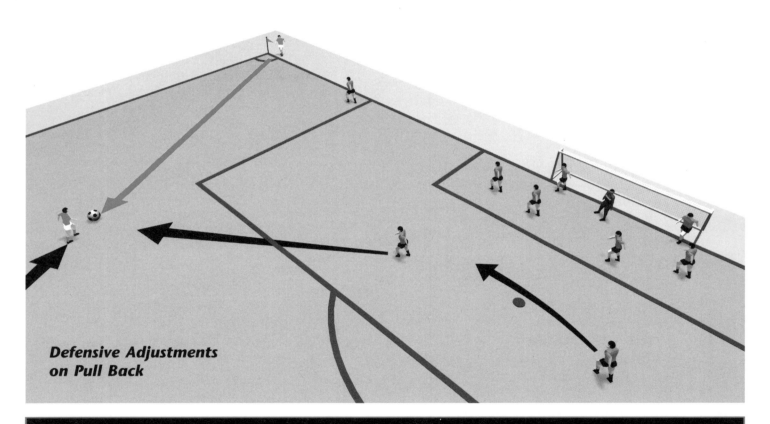

**Defensive Adjustments
on Pull Back**

DON'T LOSE YOUR HEAD!

Some of the top pro and college teams are fortunate to have portable Free Kick devices they can quickly convert into 2-man, 3-man, 4-man or 5-man walls. Sure beats getting your own players in there with soccer ball missiles whipping around them, above them…and at them!

While I was the head coach at Plymouth Argyle, in the '70s, Jim Furnell — our goalkeeper and assistant coach — was, and I guess still is, a handy man. At a staff meeting, when discussing Free Kick practice, we said it would be great to have a practice wall. "I can do that," said Jim.

And he did.

Using 5-ply wood, he built a 4-man wall, with a hinged extra "man" to make the optional 5-man wall. It looked great. So out on to the field we went. The first bending Free Kick from our dead ball specialist, Steve Davey, was slightly off target and caught the head of the end man, who was immediately decapitated! Oh, well! We tried!

Attacking Free Kicks

As we said in the Introduction, Free Kicks for the attacking team, particularly in the Front Third, always present an opportunity to score. The attacking team, in its own time, can position players in the most effective positions to increase the chances of scoring. Certain time limitations will be imposed by the referee, but a well-organized and well-rehearsed team can reposition any player without upsetting the referee.

Always keep this advantage in mind, unless your team is leading by one or two goals with the clock running down. In that case, the team may elect not to incur the risk of bringing good defenders forward and out of their most effective defending positions when, barring mistakes, the game is already won.

As the best scoring opportunities occur in the final third of the field, that's where the concentration will be in this chapter. However, Free Kicks in the Back and Middle Thirds present a very real opportunity to penetrate the Front Third on your own terms and, therefore, must be practiced.

ATTACKING FREE KICKS IN THE BACK THIRD

See the illustration on the next page.

The thinking here should be:

1. **Can you play it early and long and get behind the opposition's back players?**

2. **Can you play it early with a long fading ball that can be accepted by one of your forward players?**

3. **Can you take a quick short Free Kick, maintain possession and catch the opposition off-guard?**

4. **Can you play it wide and early or switch it quickly to the other side of the field and mount an attack from the flanks?**

5. **If the early opportunity has gone, then you can begin the setting up of a rehearsed Set Play.**

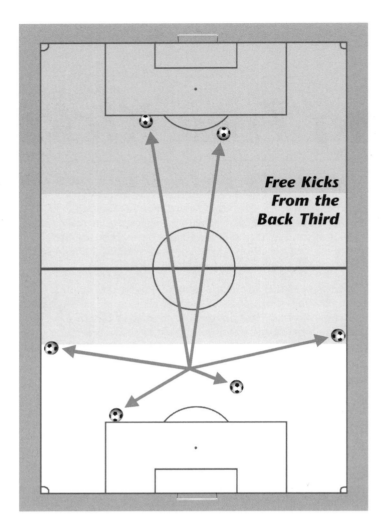

Free Kicks From the Back Third

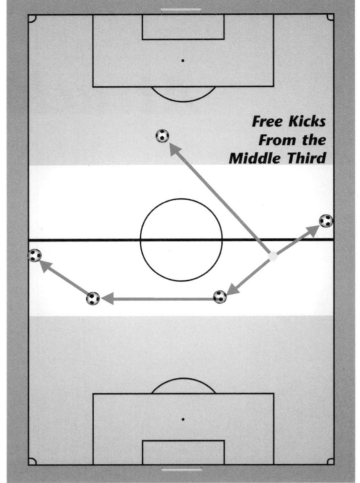

Free Kicks From the Middle Third

Remember, in the Back Third, the first consideration is safety. A team must not chance giving the ball away in the Back Third, which is, after all, is the opponents Front Third!

MIDDLE THIRD

The thinking is similar to the Back Third, but in more positive and optimistic terms. Making a mistake here will be less costly than the Back Third, but some caution must be used. So the questions are:

1. **Can a quickly taken Free Kick penetrate the defense and generate a scoring opportunity — such as playing a telling chip ball in behind the defense and/or into the penalty area?**

2. **Can a quickly taken, short Free Kick give possession against an unsuspecting and unprepared defenders to present a number of opportunities — such as running at the heart of the defense?**

3. **Can you go wide and get in behind the defense?**

If none of the above appears to present an immediate opportunity, a rehearsed Free Kick is the next option. Delaying the Free Kick may be needed to allow key players to take up their positions of maximum effectiveness for the Set Play.

In the case of the rehearsed Set Play, the players should try to avoid alienating the referee as the kick is being set up. Also, the player(s) on-the-ball should always retain the option of taking a quick Free Kick if there are lapses of concentration by the opposition (note of caution: Taking a quick Free Kick as back defenders are moving up for the rehearsed Free Kick could cause major problems if the ball is lost to the opposition).

FRONT THIRD

This is where the excitement intensifies if you're attacking and where anxiety can run rampant if you're defending.

In fluid play, positive players prepared to take risks will draw Penalties and Free Kicks from frantic defenders — without the necessity for cheating.

There are four main areas for Free Kicks in the Final Third. Please note the area out towards the corner in the deepest part of the field. While these are good attacking positions, we are going to treat them as we would "Corners Kicks" (see Chapter 2, Attacking Corners).

Take a look at the illustration at the top of the next page.

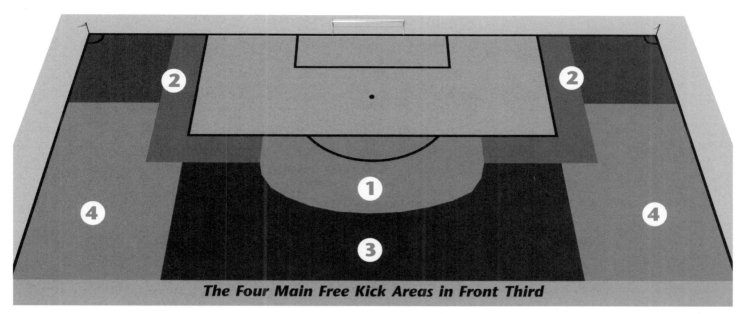

The Four Main Free Kick Areas in Front Third

WIDE IN THE FRONT THIRD (Area 4)

Certain "golden opportunities" apply in these situations:

1. **Try to put two players on the ball.**

2. **If the defending team leaves this 2-vs-1, consider getting in behind the defense in wide positions (below).**

3. **Look at the defenders' line of defense (following page). Is it too close to the goalkeeper? Too far out? Defense too close? Too far out? Just right?**

4. **Is the goalkeeper too far off the goal line? Too far back from the Near Post? Too far forward of the Near Post?**

The execution and rehearsed Set Play will depend almost entirely on the players you have and the way your opponents defend.

The diagram on the following page shows the three most common options and considerations that you as the coach must help exploit.

1. Defense too close

 a. Ball played into the mixer for "fight" in the six-yard box; look for rebounds and gifts.

 b. Runs to the Near and Far Posts; Outswinger or Inswinger

 c. Short and/or square in front of the deep defense.

2-vs-1 on the Flanks

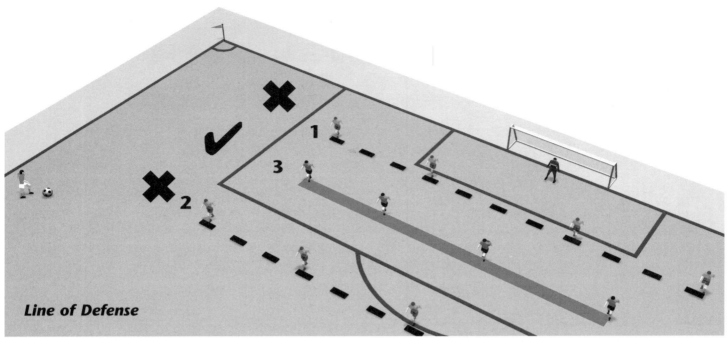

Line of Defense

2. Defense too far out

Outswinger splits the difference between the goalkeeper and the back defender(s). Inswinger must be bent over the penalty spot and just over the defense — otherwise it's easier for goalkeeper and difficult for Near/Far Post runner to "time" contact.

3. Line of Defense just right

Even if the defenders appear to have it right (as below), they're still in a most vulnerable and penetrable position, but the execution has to be more accurate. Because of the poor defensive positions in the first two examples, any type of ball into the "mixer" or just behind a defense pushed up too high is going to cause problems.

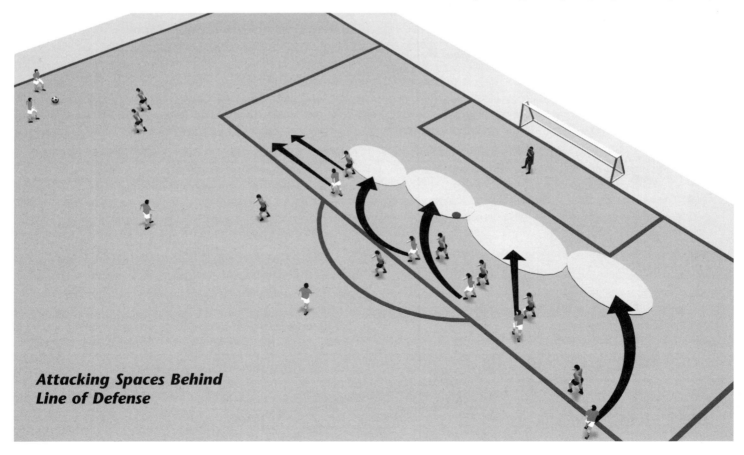

**Attacking Spaces Behind
Line of Defense**

In all three examples, both the Inswinging and Outswinging wide Free Kicks are very effective.

The Outswinger is bending in towards the incoming attacking players, making it an easier contact and providing "power" — usually, but not always, by the head.

The Inswinger makes the timing of the run and contact with the ball more difficult, but it's difficult for the goalkeeper to judge or read, and the slightest deflection means little reaction time and may leave the goalkeeper on the wrong foot. Again the head is the principal contact weapon, but a touch or volley by the foot may do just as well with a dropping ball.

The coach must assess who his best executors (EXO) are and put the players in their most effective positions (Square Pegs).

On these wide Front Third Free Kicks, Fakes and Distractions (FADS) are effective in ensuring the spaces chosen for exploitation (EXO) are emptied of potentially space-marking defenders.

For instance, if a critical space for the rehearsed Free Kick is being marked by a defender, then an attacking player moves into the space in front of the space marker and drags him or her out — just as the kick is to be taken — by making a short run (FAD) towards the ball (see illustration on previous page). This also helps distract other opponents and confuses their concentration (AAA).

There's much more to these Free Kicks from wide positions in terms of the "runs" and the "garbage goals" and the "rebounds," but that will be covered in more detail in the Free Kicks from the angles of the penalty area and those from the central area in front of the goal (Areas 1 and 2). The principles and methods recommended for Areas 1 and 2 should be applied for the wide Free Kicks (Area 4).

CENTRAL FREE KICK POSITIONS ON ENTRY TO THE FRONT THIRD (Area 3)

These Free Kicks are frequently conceded as defending teams strive, sometimes desperately, to prevent opponents from getting into the shooting zone. In most cases, the distances are too far out from goal (30 to 35 yards) to justify a direct shot on goal — unless the opposition, in its wisdom, decides to put up a two- or three-man wall, which screens the keeper. A swerving, dipping shot around the outside of the wall may blindside and wrong-foot a goalkeeper (see "No Wall Outside The Box" page 46).

There are three main options open on these type of Free Kicks:

1. If the defense drops towards the keeper, a quick short Free Kick may present a 2-on-1 or a chance to run at the heart of the defense with "give-and-go's" and other worthwhile gambles available.

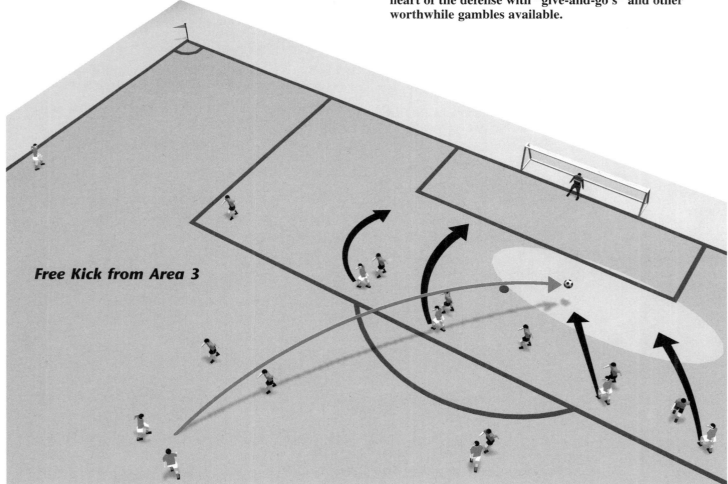

Free Kick from Area 3

2. **The ball can be played wide and present an opportunity either for getting behind the defense or sending a telling cross into the heart of the scoring zone.**

3. **If the defense sets up its line of defense somewhere but the penalty spot and the top of the box — as many teams do — the Far Post space becomes available and attractive for a well-rehearsed Set Play, as in the diagram on the previous page.**

The ball is played — Inswinger or Outswinger — into the space shown. The kick needs to be high enough to clear the defense, but not so high it floats for too long. Nor should it be over-hit, making the timing of runs difficult and more favorable for the goalkeeper.

Most times, the ball will be "bumped" by the head across the face of the goal and towards what is now the Far Post for a teammate to strike at goal.

From more central positions the ball in is angled more and the "runners" start from wider positions to make initial heading contact.

POSITIONS AT THE SIDES AND THE ANGLES OF THE PENALTY AREA (Area 2)

Many Free Kicks are conceded in the areas around the sides and angles of the penalty area. Desperate challenges motivated by a compelling desire to stop players entering the penalty area — one way or the other! — produce a high incidence of opportunities from these positions.

Usually, teams will put at least two players in the wall in these areas and sometimes as many as three or four, as the Free Kick area moves towards the top of the box and around the angle towards the center.

The purpose of a wall is to make it more difficult to hit a powerful direct shot at goal (both from a direct Free Kick and a touch-and-shot indirect Free Kick). It also presents an opportunity. The wall either blinds the goalkeeper, or forces the goalkeeper towards the Far Post to see the ball. Either way, the keeper is vulnerable.

The wall and viewing position expose the goalkeeper to a direct, inswinging chipped/swerve shot or a touch pass to the right and a power strike just inside the Near Post. Percentages of success increase as a mis-hit shot can fool and wrong-foot the keeper and rebounds are always likely.

Much depends on how the defenders arrange themselves. For instance, closer to the goal line, they may decide to defend the goal similar to a Corner Kick and put players on each post. The situation changes, but the principles don't. It allows the attacking team to put players right in the six-yard box and on top of the goalkeeper where a well-executed Inswinger (or Outswinger) will only require the merest deflection to score. Or in the confusion, and with fakes and distractions, the ball may go into the net directly from the kick.

So the alternatives from these positions are many. First of all, consider putting two players on the Free Kick — a left-footer and a right-footer — to give the options of the Inswinger and Outswinger and deceive the opposition as to who's taking the kick (FADS).

Consider extending the wall with a screen player to blind the keeper, as in the diagram on the top of the next page. There are many attractive opportunities available:

1. **Touch to the side of the wall to shoot for the open post (usually the Near Post) or dribble nearer and shoot.**

2. **Chip/swerve the ball into and just under the bar of the open post (usually the Near Post).**

3. **Inswinging cross to the Near Post for header.**

From One Angle of the Penalty Area

Screen Player Blinds the Keeper

4. Inswinging ball to and beyond the Far Post for a header.

5. Outswinging the ball to Near or Far Post.

6. Driving ball across the goal for touch in.

7. Pull back to the top/center of penalty area for late run from the back.

All of the above plays are greatly assisted by fake (FADS) runs. For instance, a run deliberately made too early to the Near Post could be the trigger for the execution of the Set Play. The early Near Post runner spins out and away, emptying the space to allow the main "executioner" of the Near Post area to move

and attack the ball coming into the empty space.

Throughout this manual, there is continuing emphasis on looking for the rebounds and garbage goals that frequently occur on Set Plays around the penalty area. Desperate, last-ditch defending, half-stops by the keeper…half-clearances from defenders…rebounds off the woodwork…all produce the "lucky goal."

The "Garbage Collector"

In the wide Free Kick situations, and at the angles of the penalty area and on Corner Kicks, the "loiterer" is a key

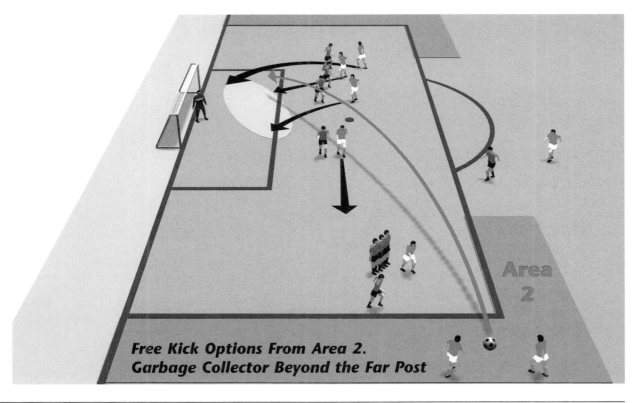

**Free Kick Options From Area 2.
Garbage Collector Beyond the Far Post**

player who — if the right player — scores from two to five goals a season.

In this example on the previous page, of the Inswinging Free Kick from the angle of the Penalty Box, the ball eludes everyone else but the "garbage collector" who coolly heads the ball in with a "thank you very much!" gesture. (see "Loitering with Intent," page 24)

So, once more, this book is not trying to produce the 2001 great Free Kicks, or the 1000 greatest Corner Kicks. Much will depend upon:

1. You, the coach.

2. The players you have — their strengths and weaknesses.

3. The response of the opposition.

Points 1 and 2 are consistent and predictable and under the control of you and your team. To a great extent, so is 3. The opposition is limited and can only do certain things.

For instance, you can predict that opponents:

1. Will come back in numbers to defend in and around the penalty area.

2. Will often try to take advantage of the offside law by setting up a line of defense.

3. Will put up a wall if the Free Kick is near the goal.

4. Must be 10 yards — probably only 9 — away from the Free Kick.

5. Will be anxious, and often agitated.

6. Don't know what is going to happen next (Hopefully you have a better chance of that than they do! Just joking!).

So, you have a great advantage. Remember the four appropriate Principles: **KISS, EXO, FADS and GIFTS.**

CENTRAL POSITIONS CLOSE TO THE PENALTY BOX (Area 1)

These positions, centrally situated 28 yards or less from goal, give the best chance of scoring from a Free Kick. I've said 28 yards or less because, as you will see in Chapter 5, I don't believe a wall is necessary from a distance greater than 28 yards. A good goalkeeper stops a shot from 28 yards or more 99 times out of a 100, if given a clear view of the ball and positioned in the center of the goal.

In the last 10 years, teams have become much better defending at Free Kicks (that's one reason why in many competitions Corner Kicks produce more goals than Free Kicks). Consequently, central Free Kick situations need and merit extra work and improved execution to take advantage of this exceptional opportunity.

In planning Free Kicks from these positions, the coach must ask these questions before going to the practice field and team meeting:

1. What exceptional strikers of the ball do we have?

2. What are they particularly good at — power striking? Chipping? Swerving?

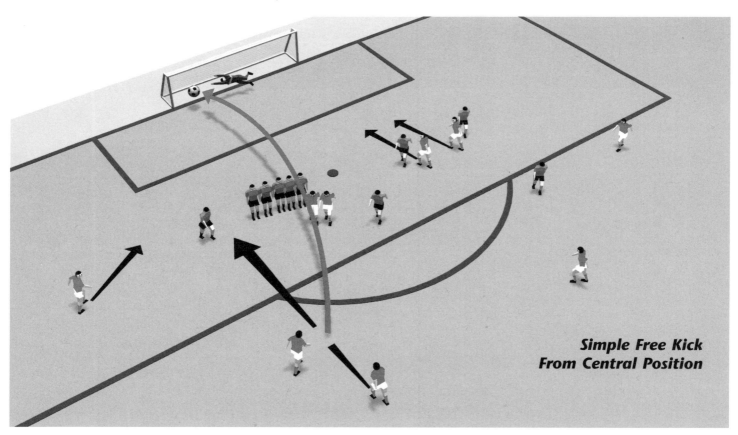

Simple Free Kick
From Central Position

3. Are these players capable of performing in "must-produce" circumstances (some may be great on the practice field and a disaster under pressure)?

4. Do we have a "leader" who can read the situations, make wise and quick decisions and help orchestrate the execution?

Once again, the **KISS** principle comes into effect. Why take a pass if one shot will do (direct Free Kick)? More than one pass on a direct or indirect Free Kick is increasing the chances of failure.

So in order to maximize the chances of scoring, a number of ploys and movements (**FADS**) are factored into the equation where optimistic, skilled runs and reactions (**GIFTS & REBOUNDS**) increase the chances of success.

Look at the methods used for the Free Kick in the illustration on the previous page:

1. **First player of the two on the ball makes dummy run over the ball as a distraction.**

2. **The two players filling in the wall do so until just before the shot is taken to affect the view of the goalkeeper. Note: The two players filling in the wall can be less than 10 yards from the ball and do not have to join the end of the wall (this upsets the defenders, who want to step forward and join them — which they are not allowed to do…i.e, the 10-yard rule!).**

3. **The most forward players off-the-ball must time their runs to stay onside, but arrive in the danger areas for the anticipated rebound off the goalkeeper or the post.**

4. **If the opposition allows a 2-vs-1 on the near side of the wall (see illustration below), the attacker nearest the wall runs away the defenders for a pass and shot for Player A. FADS at work, but remember the KISS principle.**

So for all of these Free Kicks in the Final Third, a wave of confidence and expectation for the attacking team comes from the territorial opportunity and the knowledge of their capabilities — heightened by belief in their organization through successful practice and rehearsal.

But – here's the big BUT – the team must remain organized (balanced) at the back to give cover (insurance) in case the play goes wrong. And everyone must be Jekyll and Hyde…expecting to score, yet ready to race back (recovery) if things don't work.

Indirect Free Kicks inside the box create all sorts of problems and opportunities — for the attacking team; much worse for the defending team. They also cause major control problems for the referee — one reason we don't see too many of them! We're going to leave this Free Kick for the Appendix. It's important teams are prepared for them, but they happen infrequently.

Look at Chapter 9 for ideas and the methodology to help in the organization and practice of Free Kicks and other Set Plays.

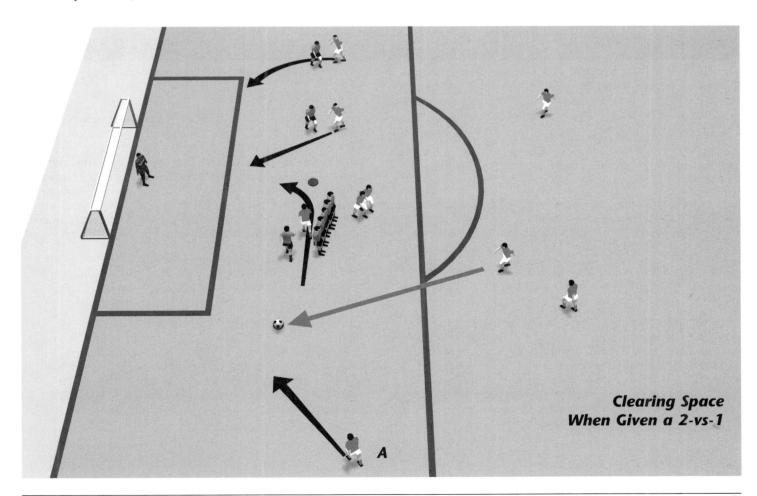

Clearing Space When Given a 2-vs-1

THE JUMPING WALL

An innovation of the '90s is the Jumping Wall.

Most teams elect to put their midfielders in their walls of three, four or five players and keep the back defenders, with the possible exception of the weakside fullback, out of the wall. That's so they can defend where they are best suited — reacting to changing situations in and around the penalty area.

Normally, midfielders are smaller than back defenders and this has created a problem in defending chipped Free Kicks. Nowadays, some teams choreograph their wall to make a collective leap just as the ball is kicked.

It certainly requires practice and the "stamp of approval" of the goalkeeper(s). Some keepers are fearful of the low shot under the wall, but that shot is difficult to execute and the goalkeeper has a full view as the wall rises.

Your call, coach. Hey! I just write books these days. I haven't used it, but I would from positions around the angles of the penalty area — providing I could convince the team and the goalkeeper it was the way to go.

CORNISH PASTIES AND DEVON DUMPLINGS

The Southwest of England, Cornwall and Devon, is a wonderful part of the world — full of folklore, tradition, great beaches, wonderful countryside and marvelous people. I wish I could be in two places at the same time!

When I first joined Plymouth Argyle in 1972, we were second-last in the Third Division. Ten weeks later, we were second-last in the Third Division! So much for my initial impact.

I knew that Inswinging Corner Kicks worked. Problem was, on Corner Kicks from the right side, we only had one natural left-footer on the team, Colin Sullivan, and he was our left back.

Should I bring him all the way from left back to what would be the right wing? Would that unbalance our defense?

After agonizing about it for a couple of weeks, I made the decision to do it. In the second half of the season, we scored eight goals from Corners, five from the right. We finished the season in the top half of the standings and were the top scoring team in our division. That gave us entry into next season's Watney Cup for the highest-scoring teams in each of the four divisions.

What a difference an extra eight goals can make!

AUTHOR'S NOTE:

Apart from the execution of the Corner Kick, we had to work hard at maintaining and restoring our team balance. Other players filled in as play continued after an "incomplete" Corner Kick. In other words, Colin Sullivan was not required back in the left-back position until there was a "natural" break in the game, such as a Throw-in, Goal Kick or Free Kick. That allowed us time to re-balance our team. Either that or we would maintain a controlled possession to allow us to re-adjust back to our regular team "shape."

Several years later, as the coach of the Canadian World Cup team, I did the same thing as we began the playdowns that eventually qualified us for the 1986 World Cup in Mexico.

Bruce Wilson, our left back and team captain, was our only left-footer in the team, so he took our Inswinging Corners from the right. In one of our first qualifying games against Guatemala, Dale Mitchell scored at the Back Post from a flick-on by Bobby Lenarduzzi at the Near Post from a perfect inswinger by Bruce Wilson. We were on our way!

Defending Free Kicks

While there may be 2001 great attacking Free Kicks, there are not many variables in defense. The No. 1 principle, after all the organization and adjustments have been made, is for everyone to be always aware and alert (Triple A's).

The defending team, by the arrangement of its players and through further adjustment (if necessary) during the pre-execution phase, does everything within its power to minimize the scoring opportunities.

When defending Free Kicks around the penalty area (Back Third), everything becomes critical. One mistake can result in a goal.

Free Kicks from the other end of the field generally require more than one mistake for a goal to be scored and normally allow the time and opportunity to remedy a mistake by one player.

DEFENDING FREE KICKS TAKEN FROM THE FRONT THIRD

There are at least four considerations to be aware of:

1. **Losing concentration (Triple A's) and being caught out, on a quick, penetrative, long Free Kick.**

2. **Allowing opponents to play easily out of their back through being outnumbered, unbalanced (2 vs 1's, etc.) unless it's the team strategy to concede high space on these Free Kicks.**

3. **Establishing the line of defense and team shape, which helps defending front players by constricting the space in which to play. This line needs adjusting as soon as the ball is in play.**

4. **Making sure, once the ball is played forward, that the ball is challenged — particularly long balls forward and especially air balls.**

Have a look at the illustration on the next page.

THE EMPERORS STRIKE BACK!

The best time to score a goal is after conceding one — not that you would want to! The momentary euphoria of success leaves the "scorers" vulnerable, celebrating their success with the inevitable complacency that goes with it! A great time to strike back. Corner Kick! Penalty! Free Kick! Own goal! Who cares?

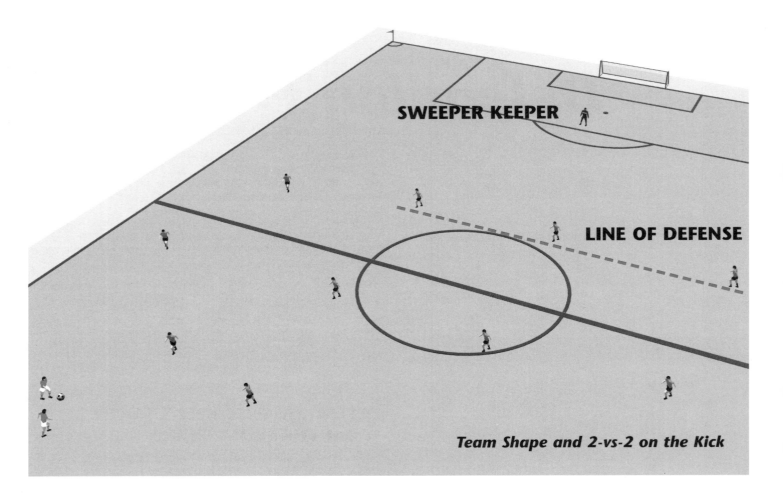

SWEEPER KEEPER

LINE OF DEFENSE

Team Shape and 2-vs-2 on the Kick

DEFENDING FREE KICKS TAKEN FROM THE MIDDLE THIRD

Penetration into your Back Third is much more likely in this area (see the illustration on the right).

Everyone should be recovering into position as quickly as possible while always remaining alert and alive (Triple A's), watching for the quick Free Kick either short, into the strikers or in behind the defense.

There are several critical situations that players must be aware of and attend to (apart from the quick Free Kick):

1. Establishing the "Line of Defense" quickly.

2. Making sure there are even numbers around the ball, ready to deal with a quick short Free Kick (i.e., 2 vs 2).

3. Keeping the defense from being blindsided by a diagonal run or diagonal ball — especially with opposing players making runs from the weak side.

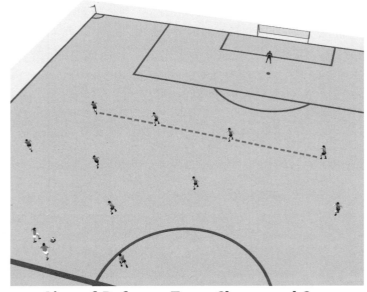

Line of Defense, Team Shape and Sweeper Keeper at Free Kicks from Middle Third

DEFENDING FREE KICKS TAKEN FROM THE BACK THIRD

As we said in the Attacking Free Kicks section (Chapter 4), the Final Third presents a great opportunity for getting a shot on goal and the defending team is understandably anxious not to make mistakes. The illustration we saw in Chapter 4 showing four critical areas for Free Kicks in the Back Third is where we'll concentrate our defensive efforts here.

It really comes down to being always alert and alive (Triple A's), both before and during the execution of the Free Kick; executing the pre-game organizational play; to making sure there are no Square Pegs in Round Holes. For instance, it doesn't make sense to bring back your 5'4" striker to defend against their 6'2" center back.

In the Back Third, the consideration before anything else — and therefore the Golden Rule — is this: "Don't give away unnecessary (make that...stupid!) Free Kicks!"

Attacking players take risks — as they should — in their Front Third. They do so by ambitious dribbling, little flicks of the ball, creative turns. When they do, it's inevitable Free Kicks will be conceded.

A defender can't lay off and not challenge indefinitely. Otherwise, opponents will waltz the ball into the net. A point of confrontation has to take place. Tackles and aerial challenges have to be made and if the timing is not quite right, or if the opposition has a "rag doll," or "how many points do I get for this dive?" Free Kicks will occur. Remember, the referee is always right — even when he is wrong! So there's no point in losing focus with overheated protests.

Giving away totally unnecessary fouls can't be condoned. But the facts are that many fouls come from genuine effort. For the coach, it is a continuing educational process — even one of indoctrination. It's a physical game and challenges must be made. There is always a fine line.

So you need aggressive defenders, who are also able to use discretion, discipline and — when the team defense is well balanced and covering the dangerous spaces — patience in the Defending Third.

So let's deal now with the Free kicks conceded (not-so-stupidly we hope) in the Back Third.

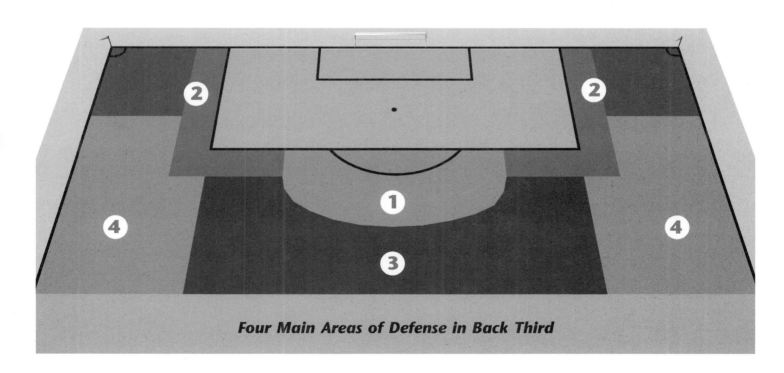

Four Main Areas of Defense in Back Third

DEFENDING FROM FREE KICKS IN WIDE POSITIONS (Area 4)

Kicks 30 yards or more from goal don't need a wall, but they do need even numbers to defend against the players on-the-ball (e.g., 2-vs-2).

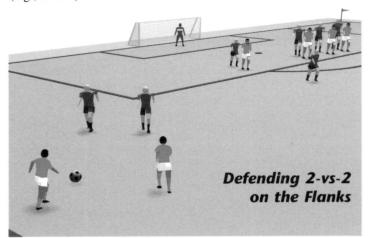

Defending 2-vs-2 on the Flanks

The distance from the ball to the goal line will determine just where the line of defense is. The nearer it gets to the goal line (12 yards or less), the more it's treated like a Corner Kick (see Chapter 3).

The goalkeeper plays a leading role in determining where the "Line of Defense" is set up (see illustration below).

"18-yard box."

"Penalty Spot!"

"Between the six-yard box and the penalty spot!"

The "Line of Defense" is critical as a start to the successful defense. The illustration below is a guide to the lines of defense from different distances from the goal line.

The coach needs to decide — with a "buy-in" from the players — if a space-marking or a man-marking system is to be used on Set Plays. Whatever the system, there are critical spaces that must be "marked" to enable defenders to be first-to-the-ball. This is accomplished by either placing players responsible for marking those spaces (Zonal Marking) or by having "man markers" arrive in those spaces before their marks (see the next page).

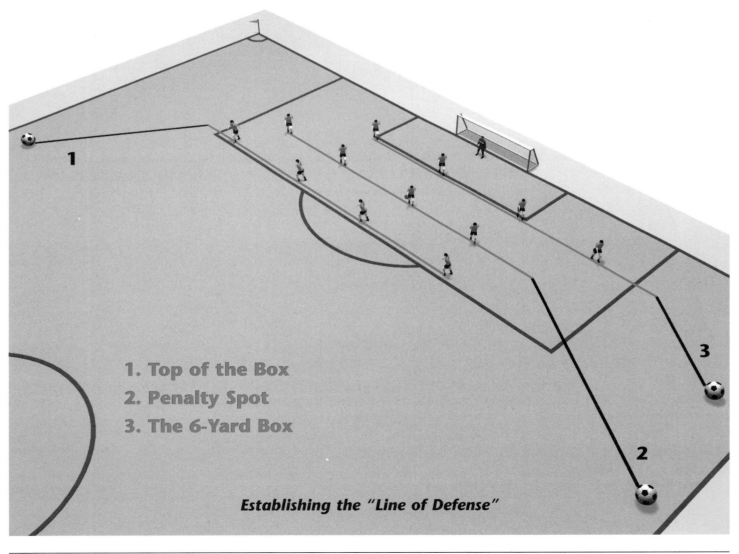

1. Top of the Box
2. Penalty Spot
3. The 6-Yard Box

Establishing the "Line of Defense"

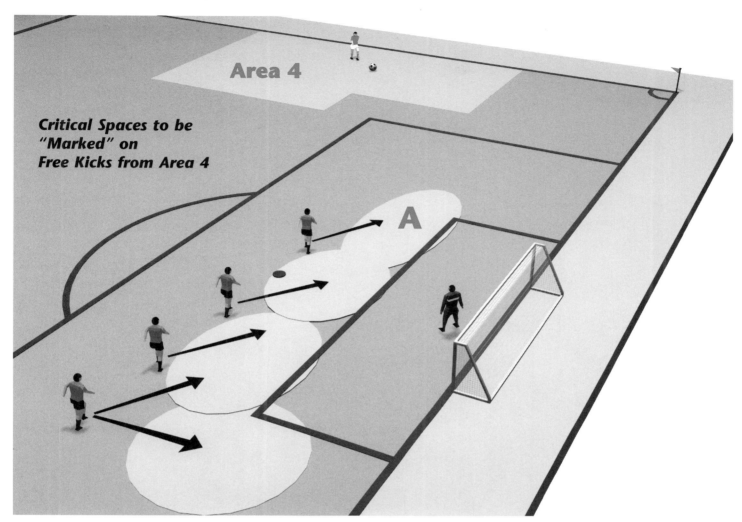

Area 4

Critical Spaces to be "Marked" on Free Kicks from Area 4

A

In all four spaces shown above, a good inswinging or outswinging ball is difficult for the goalkeeper to deal with, especially if it's not floated, thus denying time for the keeper to come out. Without allowing my own personal preference to kick in (if you'll pardon the pun!), the four spaces shown could be assigned to the best-equipped (Square Pegs in Square Holes) players. Of course, they won't stand in those spaces because the line of defense is pushed out to take advantage of the offside rule, but they can defend those spaces from their starting bases.

The diagram is only a guide — paper is not the same as grass! You need to work with your players to determine exactly where the line of defense should be. It's unlikely to be exactly as suggested here, but it won't be far off!

Whether employing a space-marking or a man-marking system, one space can't be ignored. The one opposite the Near Post (shown in the diagram as Zone A). It's my recommendation that this space is "marked" even if using a man-marking system. A good attacker, by timing and "FADs," may well arrive in that space before a marking player. In Chapter 4, we suggested that when attacking, if this space is being marked, try to move the space marker out of it. This is the tit-for-tat mentality that must go on in soccer. The space marker is reluctant to be drawn away from that space no matter what FADs are going on.

CENTRAL FREE KICK POSITIONS ON ENTRY INTO THE BACK THIRD (Area 3)

As we pointed in the previous chapter, these Free Kicks are often conceded as teams strive to prevent opponents from getting into the shooting zone. Distances of 30 to 35 yards are too far out to justify a direct shot on goal (see "No wall outside the box" on the next page).

As soon as a Free Kick is conceded, the defense must get organized quickly to:

1. **Prevent a quick, short Free Kick as the attackers attempt to exploit a not-yet-organized defense (usually requires two players right and left of the ball).**

2. **Prevent an easy ball from being played wide that gives the attackers the opportunity of either getting in behind the defense or sending a cross into the heart of the scoring zone.**

3. **Set up its line of defense, while 1 and 2 are being taken care of, somewhere around the penalty spot, depending on the distance of the Free Kick from goal (see illustration on previous page).**

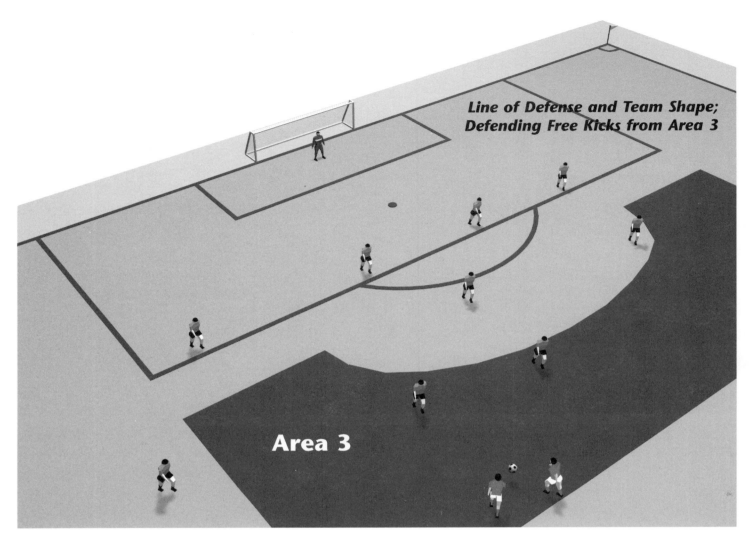

Line of Defense and Team Shape; Defending Free Kicks from Area 3

Area 3

The goalkeeper plays a leadership role here and positions off the line to shorten the distance to the back line, while at the same time avoiding being exposed to a chip shot.

The spaces identified to be exploited in the Attacking Chapter are now the spaces to be defended by the line of defense (See Chapter 4, page 35). At the risk of being repetitious, it's critical to put defenders in their most effective defending positions. For instance, a big central defender is most needed on balls played into the Far Post areas, while a shorter, determined player can do a good job marking space for the Near Post balls.

Nothing can be assumed by any defender and the play continues until what was the defending team has clear possession or the ball has gone out of play.

NO WALL OUTSIDE THE BOX

In my early years of coaching at the Pro level, I was required to learn many lessons quickly. You had to, just to survive. I was only fired once. It is an experience and a qualification. It goes on my resume! If it had happened three or more times, it wouldn't be on my resume!

In 1973, when I was the Manager/Coach of Plymouth Argyle,

we were playing our arch-rivals, Bristol Rovers. They had two scoring machines up front, Alan Warboys and Bruce Bannister, nicknamed Smash and Grab — 'cause that's what they would do.

On this particular evening, in a league game at Plymouth, they were awarded a Free Kick, 30 yards from goal. We put up a three-man wall. Warboys swerved it around the outside the wall and into the top corner of our Near Post. Jim Furnell, our very good goalkeeper, was left "painting the sky." It didn't look good.

"What happened?" was my question to Jim, after the game.

"I didn't see it until it came past the wall and I had to be at center goal to see the ball."

"What would have happened if we didn't have a wall?" I asked.

"I would have saved it easily!"

From then on in, and to this day, I've never allowed a wall to be set up outside the Penalty Box. We've always spent time on the various practice fields around the world to reassure players on the different teams I've been involved with that this is a better way to go.

Our reasoning is logical. Any wall outside the 18-yard box is 28 yards — maybe 27 yards, if the referee is being lenient! My feeling, endorsed by Jim Furnell, is that if a goalkeeper can see a shot coming from 27 yards, and can't save it, he or she doesn't deserve to be a pro goalkeeper.

And that's that. For over 20 years, that's been my team "rule." No walls outside the box!

Most attackers, when they see the open goal from that distance, wind themselves up for an almighty powerful shot on goal. Most go over the bar or past the post.

The lack of a wall outside the box has cost us one goal. That was in El Salvador, with the Canadian Olympic team in 1991. A powerfully struck shot was on its way to the terraces behind the goal when it struck one of our players, defending at an angle outside the line to the goal, and ricocheted into the path of a surprised Salvadoran making a forward run who slotted it home.

Don't let me convince you. If you think it has merit, go on the field and let players take shots on your keeper from 27 yards, and see how many goals are scored.

POSITIONS AROUND THE ANGLE OF THE PENALTY AREA (Area 2)

Many of the Free Kicks conceded in the Final Third come in the areas around the angles of the Penalty Box. Why? Because attackers are trying to penetrate the penalty area with dribbles and passes, and because last-ditch defending by players is a better gamble outside of the box than inside. Even though we don't want to concede Free Kicks, a Free Kick from outside the box is always less successful than Penalty Kicks.

As we've already said, but it's worth repeating, giving away stupid, clumsy Free Kicks and Penalties by reckless, undisciplined defenders can't be tolerated. Players who behave like that on a regular basis should not be defenders, and unless they have some other special qualities, probably shouldn't be on your team. But inevitably, Free Kicks will be played for and conceded in the areas shown.

What has to be done?

Look at the example shown below.

1. **As quickly as possible, defending players — probably all players with perhaps one exception left upfield — need to recover to help prevent a scoring opportunity.**

2. **The keeper decides (from pre-game organization/ practice) how many should go in the wall — 2, 3 or 4 (the team should know by pre-arrangement who goes in the wall).**

3. **The keeper (from pre-game agreement) decides the line of defense (e.g., two yards outside the six-yard box)...or whether to defend as a corner (i.e., two players on the post and the opposition invited to camp in the six-yard box — still with a two man wall). Personally, I would be cautious about "playing it as a corner" until the Free Kick is within 10 yards of the goal line.**

4. **The coach and the players agree on the strategy for defending at the Free Kick — space-marking or a man-marking. However, the areas shown in the diagram on the next page are the most critical.**

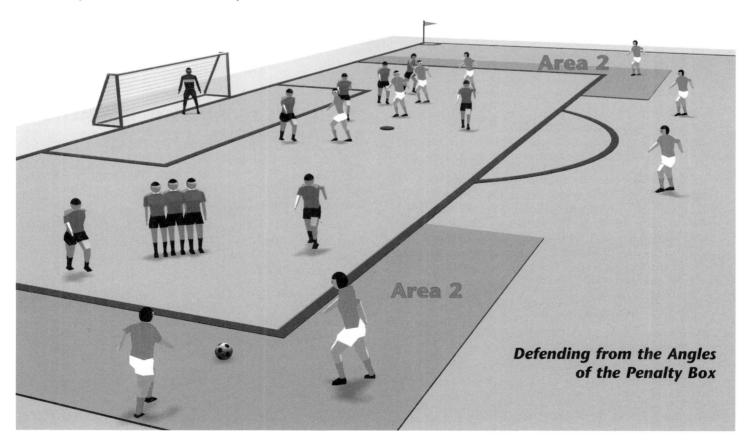

Defending from the Angles of the Penalty Box

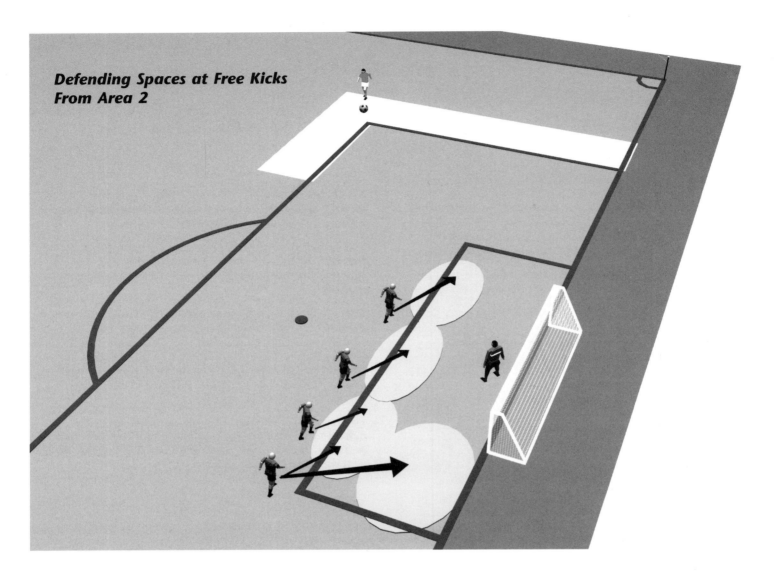

Defending Spaces at Free Kicks From Area 2

Do you mark space or mark players who may go into those spaces? I have always marked "space," but it's your call. Whatever the decision, make sure your players are capable of arriving in these dangerous spaces before the opposition.

5. **If the opposition "fills the wall" as we've suggested in Chapter 4, page 37, it can make things much more difficult for the keeper, who now can't see the ball unless he/she moves towards the Far Post. This makes the keeper more vulnerable to a Near Post inswinging chip shot or cross. Note: There is no benefit in marking the attacking "screen" player as it loses a defender to a "nothing role" and further impedes the vision of the keeper.**

Of course, there are variations to the Free Kicks and that's where our 12 Key Principles of Set Plays comes into play. All defenders need to be always alert and alive (Triple A's), ready to react to whatever happens.

FREE KICKS FROM CENTRAL POSITIONS AROUND THE PENALTY AREA (Area 1)

We've already said that in the Final Third central position from 28 yards and out, there is a strong case for not having a defending wall. And that at all times we need a well-balanced and attentive (Triple A's) defense.

Most goals on Free Kicks come from within 10 yards of the Penalty Box. A shot on goal from 28 yards or less gives the opposition a great chance of scoring — unless the defense is well-organized and reacts well.

In recent years, fewer goals have been scored from these central positions. Why? Teams are much better organized and rehearsed in correctly reacting to these situations. Your team better be one of them, if you're going to reduce goals scored from these situations.

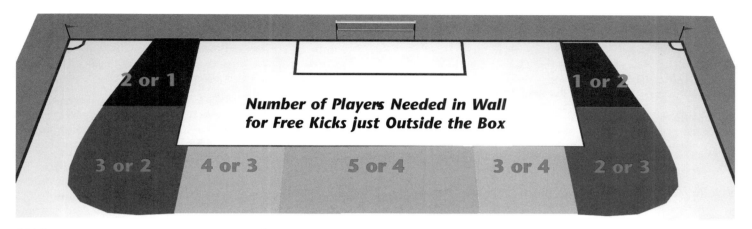

Number of Players Needed in Wall for Free Kicks just Outside the Box

2 or 1   1 or 2

3 or 2   4 or 3   5 or 4   3 or 4   2 or 3

WALL-TO-WALL DISASTER!

The scene was the Maracana Stadium, Rio de Janeiro, 1964. Brazil vs England. The stadium was only two-thirds full — 130,000 fans. It was my second start for England and we were facing the great Pele — and the rest! I had made my debut for England a week earlier in Dublin, against the Republic of Ireland and things had gone well. We won 3-1. In their wisdom (or otherwise), the English Football Association decided to fly from Dublin to New York on the Tuesday, play the United States on the Wednesday (at Randell's Island…Gordon Banks was in goal, and we won 10-0) and then fly us overnight on the Thursday to Rio de Janeiro. We arrived Friday morning for a Saturday game. Great preparation!

No, I'm not preparing our or my excuses! For 60 minutes, we competed with the Brazilians. It was 1-1. We were doing well. I was doing well. Then the floodgates opened. We ran out of steam. Brazil ran up the score. It finished 5-1.

I was held totally accountable for one of the goals. It was a Free Kick and it was the third and pivotal goal. Alf Ramsey (who became Sir Alf for his accomplishments) decided that with the Brazilians' being so lethal at Free Kicks around the box, we needed six players in the wall. On this particular Free Kick, from a slight angle off the central "D" and with a six-man wall, it was impossible for me to see the ball without being almost at the Far Post. Suddenly there was a "swiiiiissssshhhhhh!"

"What the &$%&* was that?" I thought. Well, it was the ball — now nestling in the back of the net!

Danny Blanchflower, the color commentator on BBC TV, crucified me for my poor positioning. It didn't do my playing career much good. But it greatly helped my coaching career.

I've never, ever allowed more than five men in a wall for a Free Kick from outside the penalty area. Why would I? And leave the goalkeeper in an impossible position? The keeper needs to see the ball and be able to cover the goal. Brazil won. England and Waiters lost. Waiters won — but only as a coach. No six-man walls ever again. And it has worked!

So how many in the wall? While six is too many, four may not be enough. It will depend on the angle to the goal. The graphic above gives a guideline to the numbers required for Free Kicks around the penalty area.

ORGANIZATION OF CENTRAL FREE KICKS AROUND THE PENALTY AREA

A Free Kick has been conceded in the central area in front of the penalty area, six yards out from the top of the penalty box. The pre-agreed strategy will depend somewhat on your system of play (4-4-2, 3-5-2, etc.). Take a look at the diagram below.

Defensive Set Up for Area 1

1. Keeper decides on numbers in the wall ("Five!"), except the wall does not assemble if — when set up — it would be outside the box.

2. The team already knows the five players who go into the wall (the midfielder and the weak-side fullback, or the five midfielders — coach/team decision).

3. The outside of the wall is defended by the right fullback (depends on your system of play).

4. The Central Defenders take up their "reactive/experienced" positions in the box.

5. A (brave) "bullet man" is needed to charge down the touch pass for a shot to eliminate the wall — whether the kick is direct or indirect. A decision is needed here as to whether the "bullet man" should come on a straight line to the ball (blocks more but impedes the view of the keeper and could lead to a difficult-to-read deflection), or from an angle which the keeper can see and read if a deflection takes place with a better chance of reacting. I favor the second position (see diagram below).

6. A team decision needs to be made as to who lines up the wall. If the goalkeeper is lining the wall at the Near Post, it leaves the keeper vulnerable to a quick Free Kick to the Far Post. However, if another player lines up the wall, does the keeper have enough confidence that the wall is right?

7. How does the wall adjust as the referee moves it back; or when the opposition craftily moves the ball one foot to the side?

Here are my observations — for what they are worth!

1. I always prefer to have the goalkeeper positioned and visually able to defend the shot — quick or not — rather than doing shuttle runs from center goal to the Near Post to ensure the wall is in place.

2. It's necessary to assure the keeper the wall is correctly in place. I assign a responsible front player on a recovery run from up field to organize the wall by aligning the last player to cover the Near Post and beyond (cover the swerve shot).

3. The outside two players covering the Near Post must be very aware of the positioning (and potential re-positioning of the wall). The outside man is positioned on a line between the ball and the post passing over on the "inside shoulder" (see below).

In today's game with inswinging, bending balls — and the ability to kick them improved by the specially-developed high-tech soccer balls — the wall needs a "man over," i.e.,…with the inside shoulder on the Near Post and the rest of the body outside the post.

So now you've got it! Or have you? Nothing is perfect and practice will increase your percentages of successfully repelling an attacking Free Kick (see Chapter 9, How to Teach & Coach Set Plays).

Our objective from a defensive perspective is to make it increasingly difficult to score. After all, isn't that the secret of winning soccer? We won't necessarily get it right every time. But the more times we get it right, the fewer the chances are of conceding a goal!

BULLET MAN

"Bullet Man" Coming from Angle Allows Keeper to See the Ball

Aligner Moves to Most-needed Position

FURTHER ADJUSTMENTS TO THE BASIC DEFENSIVE ORGANIZATION ON CENTRAL FREE KICKS IN FRONT OF THE GOAL

Four-man wall vs five-man wall. Who is the "fifth man?"
(Answer: weak-side fullback or weak-side wide midfield player — depends on system and whether there are four or five midfielders.)

What does the "fifth man" do if not required in the wall?
(Answer: works at the direction of the central defenders and the keeper.) For example:

With only four in the wall, the spare (fifth) wall player could neutralize a 2-vs-1, producing a 2-vs-2 on the near side of the wall, or assist the two central defenders at the far side of the wall (Triple A's).

These are critical, quick and final adjustments that the defending team needs to be aware of just before the kick.

As well, if a recovering forward is responsible for initially lining up the wall, where does he or she go after doing that from a position behind the ball? (Answer: where the greatest danger is.). For example:

1. If there are five in the wall and the attacking team tries to overload the near side to produce a 2-vs-1, the "aligner" goes to assist the space-marking defender outside the Near Post wall player.

2. Or if a ball played square inside for a central shot appears to constitute the greatest danger, the aligning/recovering forward (the "aligner" repositioned at Point A) takes that position — especially if there is not a 2-vs-1 by the wall.

The following factors are determined on the practice field and will not vary too much:

• **The goalkeeper's position.**

• **Who goes in the wall?**

• **How many go in the wall?**

• **Who lines up the wall?**

• **Who is the bullet man and does he/she approach from straight on or at an angle?**

While "decisions-of-the-moment" can be anticipated and planned, there is always something that can go wrong. Each of the 11 players has a specific job and all 11 need to do their jobs collectively and harmoniously. Because one gets it wrong doesn't necessarily mean the whole organization breaks down. But it does mean nothing is assumed. The Triple A's principle (Always Alert and Alive) is paramount once the defending team is well-organized.

Finally, reactions, rebounds and repositioning will all be considerations once the ball is in play.

HITTING THE WALL! THE WHITE FEATHER SYNDROME!

There are a few "jobs" in soccer that no one relishes. One is the Bullet Man on Free Kicks (see page 50). Another is being a member of "the wall." The task of the wall is, physically, to prevent the opposition from taking a free shot on goal. The "bodies" of the wall are the only physical obstacle for the opposition. Everything may depend on the efficiency of the wall to stop the cannon ball that is being smacked towards them...and stop the goal.

Anything that can help the solidarity of the wall and alleviate the anxiety — fear! — of the wall members must be encouraged and practiced.

For instance, linking arms as some walls do is not recommended. It holds the wall in position long after the kick has been taken. Even worse, it commits both arms into the linking and leaves the "family jewels" exposed (this is a somewhat sexist thing, but you'll get the drift as we go along!).

The following recommendations will help:

1. Only one hand is used to protect the family jewels. Unless I've totally misread the situation, one hand is enough. Sorry to be a little facetious here as I know this is serious stuff. But I'm only trying to help!

2. The other hand, working from the outside man in (i.e., the player covering the outside the Near Post to prevent a swerved shot) grasps the outside seams of the shorts of the player next to him (or her) to pull the colleague close and consolidate the wall (see photo). If and when the wall needs to break, the shorts-grip is automatically sprung as a player breaks away.

3. Even though the body is held upright to maximize the height of each person, the chin is pulled in and the head angled down, with the eyes looking at the ball. In the photograph, the players are not doing this to the extent they should and could be struck in the face. Tilting the head helps prevent the ball striking the nose while not significantly reducing the height of each player. Should a ball hit the head of a player in the wall, it has a greater chance of striking the forehead rather than the face and the forehead is better able to deal with the impact.

The Jumping Wall which we have discussed (on page 40) can increase the effectiveness of the wall. Being a wall member is not one of soccer's most attractive jobs, but someone has to do it. And we don't want to see the ball in the net and a couple of white feathers on the floor where the wall used to be!

Political correctness prevents me from going into some of the volatile locker room inquests I've been involved in after someone "chickened out" on a defensive Free Kick. Suffice it to say that at the pro level with livelihoods on the line, the accusations and observations wouldn't go over well at a church party.

YOU'RE THE COACH

All players have their personal favorite Free Kick. And you can bet your bottom dollar they'll be at the center of it! You can also pretty well guarantee the plays will be creative — and complicated!

You are the coach! You have to bring the team together — one way or the other! You have to convince the players (while respecting their egos) that there are some (simple) effective ways of capitalizing on Set Plays.

This is the management aspect of obtaining Set Play consensus within the team.

Throw-ins

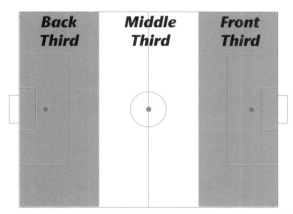

As with Free Kicks, much depends on in which third of the field the throw is taken:

Back Third — No-nonsense, safety first area.

Middle Third — Requires some caution. Possession is the key unless the throw can go directly into the Top Third.

Front Third — Area to be creative and to take higher risks both with planned and unplanned "percentage" plays.

THROW-INS FROM BACK THIRD

1. **A quick Throw-in to an unmarked, unpressured player (including the goalkeeper) is the way to go. If pressure is imminent, the ball can be quickly transferred to the other side of the field or played forward safely into the Front Third.**

Throw to Unmarked Player

2. **The throw for a return to an unmarked, and clearly unpressured, thrower results in good possession in the Back Third. Note (see illustration on next page) that the throw can be made to the head, but is often more effective to the foot as**

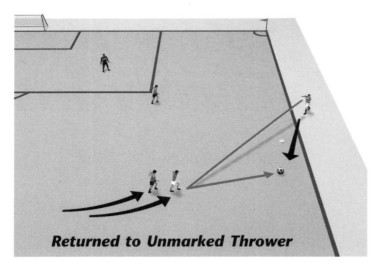

Returned to Unmarked Thrower

the player comes towards the thrower. Then it's easier for the thrower to receive the ball as it will not be bouncing and coming back from a height.

3. If all simple outlets are threatened, then the "throw-down-the-line" will work nine times out of 10. We'll deal with that as we move into the Midfield Third.

MIDDLE THIRD

1. A quick throw — perhaps a long Throw-in to the Attacking Third — is always the preference. Penetrating the Final Third is always be the No. 1 consideration. Maintaining possession is a close second.

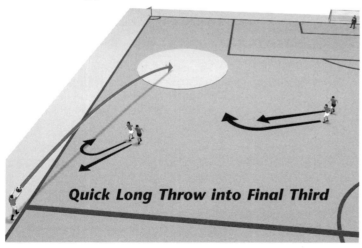

Quick Long Throw into Final Third

2. A more prepared long throw over a forward player for a second player to run on to, and so penetrate into the Front Third, is a great play. It's well worth the gamble, particularly with an accomplished and accurate long-throw specialist.

3. The throw for the return ball for a unmarked, and clearly unpressured, thrower results in good possession in the Middle Third in the same way it does in the Back Third (see "Unmarked Thrower" at top of page).

DOWN THE LINE

From the Back Third through the Middle Third — even entering into the Front Third — you can pretty well be guaranteed of maintaining possession or of winning another Throw-in (or Free Kick) from a Throw-in "down line" — providing the play is practiced and understood.

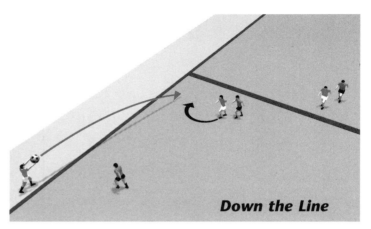

Down the Line

With other outlets such as the ball to the goalkeeper denied, or with a simple throw to an unmarked defender not available, or with the thrower marked to prevent a return pass, the best play is the down-the-line Throw-in. It always provides a safe option and usually allows you to progress from the Back Third to the Front Third with a succession of Throw-ins.

In the illustration above, you see that the receiver of the ball doesn't take away his or her space by coming to close to the touchline. Four yards from the touchline is a good rule of thumb.

It's also important that the receiver is not too close to the thrower, but nor too far away…10 or 12 yards is a good guide.

Most defenders at this distance mark from behind and on an inside line to the goal, allowing free space between the receiver and the touchline.

The thrower must deliver a good ball down the outside of the receiver, for the receiver to move into and control, and screen from the marking defender. A ball that bounces a yard or two in front of the receiver, that can be controlled by the stomach, works well — as the ball can be screened and the controller can turn out along the touchline. Most defenders attempt to challenge as the receiver turns to go down the line and often kick the ball out of play for another Throw-in. If they fail to challenge, then the receiver can dribble forward close to the line, with the body between the ball and the defender, inviting another challenge and the very real chance of another Throw-in — or a Free Kick!

Two or three throws later, and your team may be in possession of a Throw-in in the Front Third.

A well-organized defending team could mark the receiving player on the "wrong side," i.e., on the outside or in front of the Receiver — particularly if they have good cover when they can double-team. This makes the throw to the first Receiver almost impossible, but opens up a great opportunity for a down-the-line throw to a second Receiver (see next page).

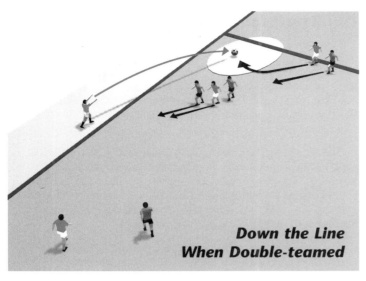

**Down the Line
When Double-teamed**

and creates more space behind for the second receiver. This is very important as the first receiver could be marked front and back, and space needs to be created for the second receiver.

There are other variations to this throw which you, as a coach, can develop. For instance, even if the first receiver is marked front and back, a lobbed throw to the head of the first receiver can be touched/flicked-on and into the path of the second receiver (see bottom left).

THE FRONT THIRD

1. This is the place to be creative, have fun and take risks. Always encourage your players to look for a quick throw that could catch the defending team unprepared and undermanned (Triple A's).

Quick Throw In Final Third

Once more, it is important the second receiver doesn't move into the outside space too early (this space will be more than four yards…more like six or seven), as it takes away the receiver's space while at the same time bringing the covering defender into a better defending position (above).

The timing of the second receiver's run, and the timing and technique of the throw, are important. With the attacker receiving the ball on the outside (between the attacker and the touchline), the defender faces a dilemma: "Should I tackle? Or should I jockey and hustle?"

Either way, as long as the dribbling player keeps the ball partially screened on the outside, there's an excellent chance of making progress forward or winning another Throw-in — or maybe a Free Kick. In fact, the receiver may let the ball run down the line and stay beside it — and therefore in playing distance — without having to do much else. This will invite the challenge and most times lead to another Throw-in.

If the first receiver is being marked on the outside or in front, just before the throw is taken, the first receiver should move towards the thrower. That brings the marker or markers forward,

2. If a defense is poorly organized without balance and cover, can you make a Throw-in to a player in a 1-vs-1 situation with the encouragement to go for goal?

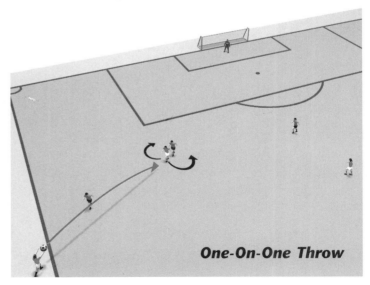

**Down the Line
Flick-on Header**

One-On-One Throw

3. If the thrower is unmarked, that's an important consideration as a quick Throw-in and pass back to the thrower gives a 2-vs-1 on the flanks in the Top Third — always a positive attacking situation (see next page).

(A) The Long Throw

Most teams will have at least one player who is good enough to reach the Near Post area with a long Throw-in (30 yards or so). If the field is narrow or you have a incredible athlete (see the American Throw on page 89) it may be possible to reach the Far Post area. The distance that can be consistently reached will be established in practice. Have a Long Throw-in competition (see Chapter 9).

The receiving player (Target Man) should be someone who's good in the air and tall (it may mean bringing up a back defender). The player can stand right in the desired space and act as a target for the thrower. Chances are that player will be marked front and back, but that's okay. The defenders may inadvertently do the job you're looking for.

The Target Man should be far enough from the goal (10 yards) to make it difficult for the keeper to come for the ball.

In this play, the Target Man is merely looking to flick the ball on with the merest touch of the ball at the hairline (or for some of us, where the hairline used to be!) and for the ball to continue in the same direction (see what we mean in the illustration below).

The player making the #1 run is anticipating (i.e., hoping and praying) that the ball is slightly over-thrown or misjudged by the defenders and Target Man and carries into the space behind them for a volley or diving header.

**Back to Thrower
In Front Third**

If the three options just shown, including the one above, are not available, your players should be encouraged to look at using a "planned" throw.

We're going to show several examples:

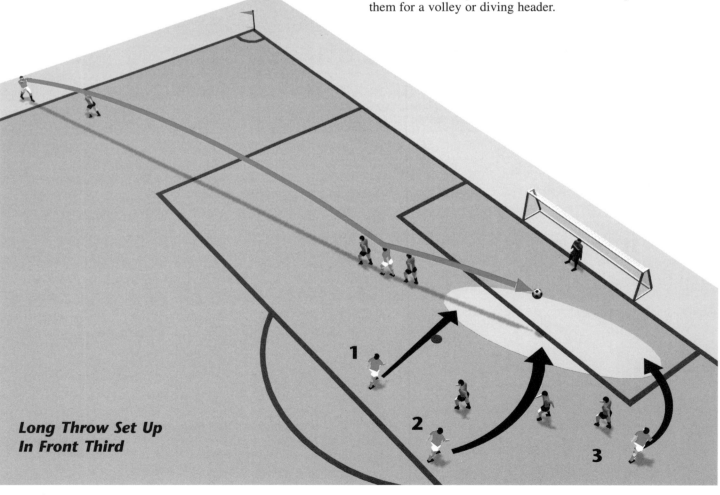

**Long Throw Set Up
In Front Third**

1

2

3

In the #2 run, the attacker is anticipating the flick-on and aims to arrive in that space at the same time as the ball — for a tap-in or volley, or perhaps a header.

The player in the #3 run is going in for the "garbage goal" that eludes everyone. He or she may have to make that run 20 or 30 times to score the goal. Gifts often have to be earned, but it will happen, sooner or later. And it will happen again!

A "ring of confidence" around the outside of the penalty area is needed to make sure that even if the defenders make a successful header clearance — "it's not over yet!"

(B) CROSS-OVER RUNS

Whatever marking system is being used in fluid play, most teams will man-mark on Throw-ins. This presents a number of opportunities for Cross-overs and Blocks.

Remember that a player receiving a Throw-in cannot be offside.

Cross-over with Space to Goal

On entry into the Front Third, and with space available towards the goal line, a Cross-over is effected by **Player 1,** running towards the Thrower. At the same time, **Player 3** takes his marker from the space we are looking to use with **Player 2.** This creates a 1-vs-1 just outside the penalty area and in a very advantageous attacking situation.

If the timing of the penetrative run is good and the defense is caught a little off guard, it may be possible to throw the ball in front of the receiver, for the receiver to make a first-time cross. Otherwise, the throw will be slightly on the outside of **Player 2** to enable the ball to be screened from a marking player. Possession is obtained in a dangerous and productive part of the field.

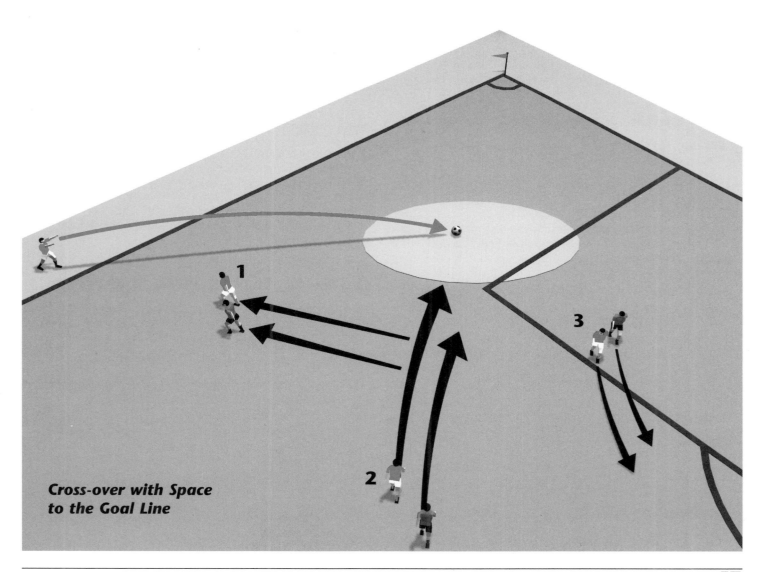

Cross-over with Space to the Goal Line

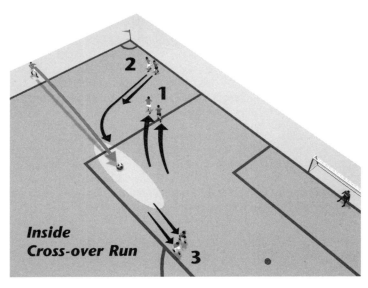

Inside Cross-over Run

Inside Cross-over Run

In the Inside Cross-over, **Player 1** starts the play by making a darting run towards the corner flag shouting for the ball (FADS). **Player 3** clears the space with a decoy run (FAD). **Player 2**, from the goal line, moves towards the thrower and then turns quickly inside.

The ball must be thrown on the outside line shown to keep it away from the marking defender. But if the throw and the timing of the run are executed well, a real opportunity is presented for a first-time strike — likely a volley after the first bounce — or a dribble to the front of the goal.

Coming from the left, make sure the receiver has a good right foot and vice-versa on the right flank.

(C) THE BLOCK

The timing of these Cross-over runs can be simplified if one player holds position and so uses himself or herself and the marker as a block.

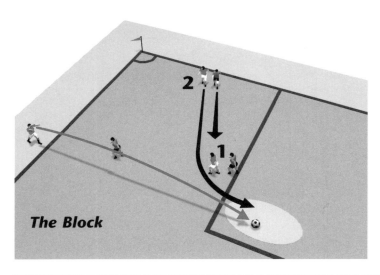

The Block

As different from the Inside Cross-over, the initial run by **Player 1** is not made. Instead **Player 1** holds position. **Player 2** comes directly back from the goal line and brushes across the front of **Player 1**. **Player 1** holds position or better still, moves a yard or so back, pushing his marker back and so opening the space for **Player 2** to move into on the turn and sprint inside. Because of the "Block", the marking defender tries to stay close or takes a wider and less-tight covering run on the angle behind the Block formed by the attacker, **Player 1,** and his close-marking defender.

Player 1 is not deliberately obstructing anyone and it does not constitute a foul. **Player 1's** passive or semi-passive role, aided by the marker, allows the opportunity for **Player 2** to shake the other marking player — or at least create more room to maneuver when receiving the ball.

The Thrower Makes The Decision

No matter what happens or doesn't happen on the Throw-in, the person in charge is the thrower. As Ronnie Moran said during my time at Liverpool: "They spoiled the game of soccer when they introduced opposition. Before then it had been easy!"

What he was really saying was that opponents don't have to respond in the way you want them to respond. It may look good in practice, but if opponents don't react the way they are "supposed" to react, the thrower has to make a decision. Throw it or not? To whom? Wait to see if there is something better? Don't wait too long — otherwise the referee may be alienated and intervene.

PRACTICE — THE KEY!

The timing and execution of Cross-over Throw-ins needs to be worked on. To get the technique and timing, it 's worth using "Shadow Practice" to get it right (see Chapter 9). Making practice realistic by putting in defenders is important, but remember they are your own team players. They know exactly what's happening so they need to be "conditioned" for the practice to succeed.

(D) FINAL 10 YARDS OF THE FIELD

A quick Throw-in for a turn or, if marked, a pass back to the unmarked thrower means great possession in a telling part of the field. But good defending teams won't let that happen often.

The Long Throw is very effective in this situation, too.

On the next page are our final two examples of simple (KISS) but effective Throw-ins the last 10 yards of the field:

1-vs-1 Turn

The receiver leaves a good five yards between him or her and the goal line. The ball is thrown to the **Receiver's** feet, and then the **Receiver** plays what is "on." Many times a defender

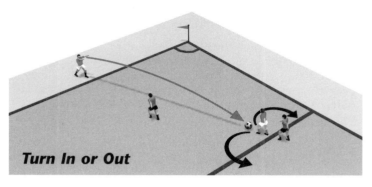

Turn In or Out

concedes a corner and then you're really in business (see Attacking Corners, Chapter 2). Most certainly the **Receiver** can gamble by turning out and dribbling along the goal line, or looking to set up the thrower or another teammate.

If the defender marks between the thrower and goal line, a ball thrown inside may create the opportunity for a hook shot or cross at goal — or a dribble at goal. Many good defending sides mark front and back in these circumstances — preventing the opportunity of the simple throw.

In these circumstances of "cat and mouse," as below, another opportunity occurs which is worth a gamble.

Long Throw — Late Run

As **Player 1** drags the two defenders towards the thrower, **Player 2** bends a run into the space for the longer throw and the flick-on, or deflection header. As a coach, you need to work with the players to establish who does what, when and where — particularly regarding the runs to meet the flick-on. The Long Throw-in described previously gives you the guide and the likely spaces that need to be attacked by the assigned players.

There are many variations to these and other throws and it's your responsibility to work out (ATDs) the most effective throws for the personnel you have (Square Pegs). And they must be practiced, if they are consistently going to provide success.

Remember too, that working a great Throw-in to get possession around the penalty area is only part of it. The attacking runs of the players not directly involved in the initial Throw-in must be right to increase the chances of scoring.

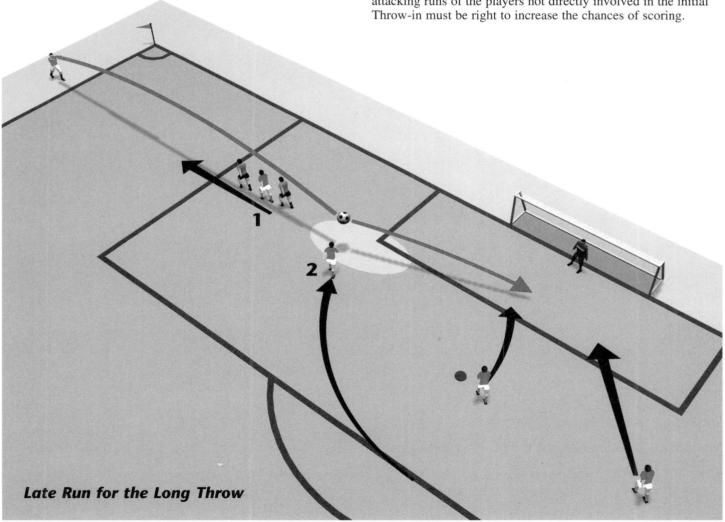

Late Run for the Long Throw

DEFENDING THROW-INS

Marking the thrower?

In the 1986 World Cup in Mexico, Canada's opening game was against France, the reigning European Champions. For little Canada, in its first World Cup ever, it was a daunting task.

Michel Platini and his cast of world-class players would walk all over Canada. Right? Not quite!

Canadian soccer's finest hour came as it stemmed the French onslaught and began to ask serious questions of France's defenders.

With 20 minutes, to go it appeared that the French were ready to settle for a tie. They hadn't broken the Canadian defense. They had tightened up their own defense. A tie for France would still be all right, considering the depth of the talent and the fact there were two more games to play in the first round.

One indiscretion changed the result. France won a Throw-in in the Top Third. The thrower was left unmarked! The ball was thrown in and returned to the thrower, who crossed to the Far Post. The ball was headed back and Jean-Pierre Papin scored. France 1, Canada 0…forever!

So should you always mark the thrower? At one time, every top team marked the thrower on the theory that it always gave an easy option to the attacking team if you didn't. Nowadays, many teams do not mark the thrower in the Defending Third and Middle Third, but most do in the Attacking Third. Personally, I would always have someone guarding against any ball back to the thrower in all thirds. Your call!

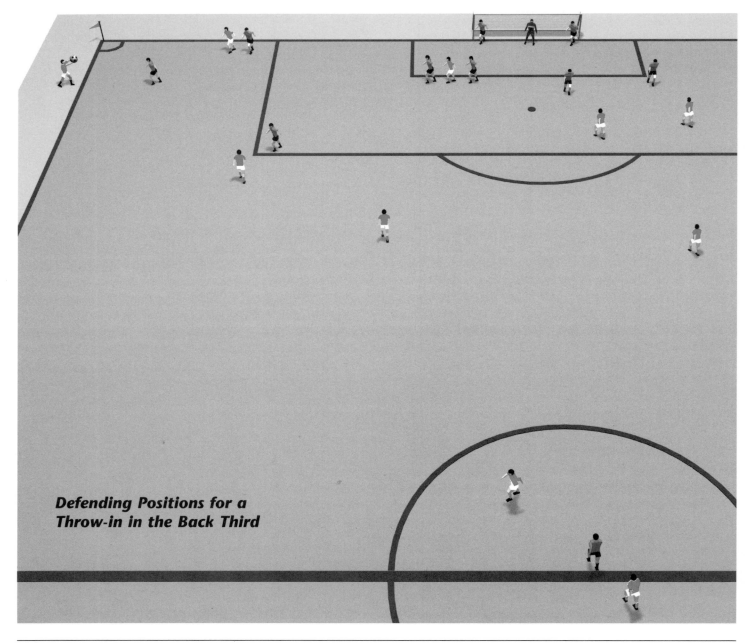

Defending Positions for a Throw-in in the Back Third

You will have already read in the Attacking Throw-in section how to counter teams that mark the **Receiver** from the front and the back at certain situations. But it is more difficult for the attacking team when that is done. So on that basis, I would recommend you consider doing just that.

When defending Throw-ins, even teams using a zonal defending system tend to mark on a man-to-man basis with players near the Thrower — and stick to them like glue.

Defending Throw-ins is not rocket science, but good basic defending keyed by having all players aware, alert and alive (Triple As).

The overall plan for the organization on Throw-ins requires pre-planning and practice. For instance, do you expect the keeper to come for the long, high Throw-in? The trajectory makes it a difficult ball to judge and catch.

Might you consider having the goalkeeper move out and mark the dangerous space for the Long Throw? Better not underestimate the Thrower!

How does a team arrange itself in and around the penalty area?

The key in defending — where there are flick-ons and crosses from Cross-overs and turns, and Long Throw-ins — is to be first to the ball and first into the dangerous spaces for crosses and passes.

If you look at the potentially dangerous spaces for the Long Throw-in or the short Throw-in in the illustrations on the previous page, you need to ensure that if the defenders challenging for the ball are beaten and the ball is crossed in or flicked-on, your own players do everything possible to get to the ball first. Note that in the illustration how the players are arranged. With the players marking the Near and Far Posts, the defending team is treating the Throw-in as they might a Corner Kick — particularly considering that on a Throw-in an attacker cannot be offside directly from the throw.

There is a strong case in these situations for a combination of man-marking the players close to the thrower, and zonal defending in the dangerous areas in front of the goal. One player (a sweeper) cannot cover all the dangerous spaces. That's your call and much depends on your players. Are they more comfortable in a man-marking system? Have they been brought up with zonal defending?

If your team is alert and alive when the ball goes dead, you won't be punished as often as the teams with poor concentration. That might sound like a BGO — a Blinding Glimpse of the Obvious — but it's a soccer fact. And players must be constantly reminded — when the ball goes dead, the mind must remain alive!

LA OLYMPICS 1984

We had beaten Cameroon in the third game of the first round of the Olympics to move on to the quarter-finals — and Brazil. The game was played at Stanford University in front of 50,000 fans.

We were playing well and ahead 1-0 midway through the second half when we were awarded a Free Kick just outside the box. Our ploy was to put two of our men, Paul James and Randy Ragan, as "extenders" to their defensive wall, to blind the goalkeeper. It worked almost to perfection. Dale Mitchell hit the shot, beat the keeper, but the ball hit the post. Ever-alert Gerry Gray, following up, side-footed the ball into the net with the keeper still on the ground.

2-0!

Or was it?

The referee was pointing to a position near the penalty spot. Offside given!

To be fair to the referee, he had taken the "offside" and delegated the goal-line position to his linesman. So he was right on the spot.

I've seen the video recording a hundred times. At the time the ball was kicked by Mitchell, all of our players were at least four feet onside, but the Brazilians froze when we followed in. It made no difference because it was no goal. The referee said so. And that's how it will always be.

Brazil tied the game and won in a Penalty Shootout after a scoreless overtime. So we didn't go to the medal round, but we did have a wonderful experience.

The irony of the story is the replay showed that it shouldn't have been a Free Kick in the first place. Randy Ragan actually tripped over the ball as he dribbled towards the penalty area. Maybe "The Man Upstairs" was having a bit of fun, but making sure justice was done! He must have a weird sense of humor!

TRICKS OF THE TRADE

Marking at the Back

On all attacking Set Plays in the Middle and Front Third, care must be taken at the back. Concentration levels must be kept high and if the opposition leaves a player or two up front, that player or players must be given the privilege of the closest marking he or she has ever had.

"Front and back!" is a common shout from the dugout as the coach insists that the lone player is double-teamed — by marking at the front and at the back of the player.

"Get inside his shorts!" is not to be taken literally! Perhaps just as well. It infers marking so close the marked player can feel and hear the breathing of the marker.

Blocking

By taking up a good attacking position close to important space, and knowing a defender must mark closely, another attacker can use the player as a "block." This is particularly effective on Throw-ins, Free Kicks and Corner Kicks in the Back Third (see Chapter 6 — Attacking Throw-ins; The Block, page 58).

Flat Runs

Timing of Runs is one of the most difficult aspects of the game of soccer. Consistently being able to time runs to arrive in the space at the same time as the ball sorts out the great players from the not-so-great.

This complex skill can be compounded by the offside law being used by the opposition for it's "Line of Defense."

With the "Line of Defense" flattened up, the runs to get to a ball in the space behind the defense not only requires great timing to avoid being ruled offside, but may have to be flattened across the line of defense before breaking through the line a split second after the ball has been kicked.

Penalties

This could be the shortest chapter in the book, but it will likely be the most important.

Many games are won and lost at Penalty Kicks — both in regular play and at Penalty Shootouts.

In most competitions today, the most goals on Set Plays are scored from Penalty Kicks. It goes without saying that they must be practiced — by both your penalty kicker(s) and your goalkeepers.

That doesn't mean non-goalkeepers and non-penalty kickers can stand around and watch (and pray) when there's a Penalty Kick. In regular play, being alert and alive (Triple A's) for the rebounds can be critical. All players must be both optimistic and pessimistic on a Penalty Kick and must believe there's a chance their intervention will be required.

"The keepers going to half stop this one and I'm going to score on the rebound!"

Or…

"It could hit the post and I could complete the clearance!"

The Penalty Kick — Everyone Alert and Alive

This is an attitude of mind that you must instill in your players.

What an incredible disappointment for the goalkeeper who makes a magnificent flying leap to fingertip the ball on the crossbar, only to find an opponent reaching the ball first and slotting it home.

As the saying goes: "Where was the goalie when the ball went in the net?"

Perhaps more pointedly: "Where were his teammates?"

At this stage, I'm not going into the best way of taking a Penalty Kick. Nor the best method of stopping a Penalty as a goalkeeper. That will depend on the abilities of your penalty kickers, your goalkeepers, your management of the practices and your judgment of the most suitable personnel.

You cannot change your keeper for a Penalty Kick — unless you do so before the end of overtime with a Shootout imminent. However, in a game there are 10 field players from whom to select your penalty kicker (and an 11th, your goalkeeper, if you really want to be bizarre!).

Obviously, good technique in the ability to strike a ball accurately, and with some pace and deception, is a key factor in your choice. But the ability to produce under pressure is probably more important.

So in practice you, as coach, must:

1. **Give ample opportunity for practicing Penalty Kicks.**

2. **Replicate the atmosphere of game circumstances as much as you are able to, by inserting some aspect of pressure. With the pros, I've put up money for the winner. That's not what you should do with 12 or 13 year olds!**

Point 2 is much more difficult to accomplish than Point 1. For penalty kickers, set up "pressure" competitions:

1. **Two shots only.**

2. **Sudden death (for all players including the goalkeepers — tournament Shootout).**

3. **Two teams (say 8-vs-8) go against each other — one kick per player — to produce a winning team (see below).**

In Penalty practice sessions, goalkeepers must be allowed to use a variety of methods to find out what works best for them.

What helps the goalkeeper is:

1. **A genuine belief in the ability to make the save.**

2. **Being alert and alive and highly motivated, but still under control.**

3. **Cultivating quick reactions rather than tipping your hand by too-early anticipation.**

Of course, prior knowledge of the penalty kicker is a huge advantage.

Goalkeeping Glory!

I had my successes at stopping Penalty Kicks. I saved two in one game from the late, great Billy Bremner of Leeds and Scotland. We still lost 4-0! And I helped get my future coaching colleague at Liverpool FC, Ron Moran, fired as the penalty kicker for Liverpool when I stopped one low with my right hand — I knew where he preferred to put them — at Anfield as Liverpool returned to the top Division in 1963. We won 2-1. Alan Ball was making his debut for Blackpool at age 17 — he won a World Cup with England three years later.

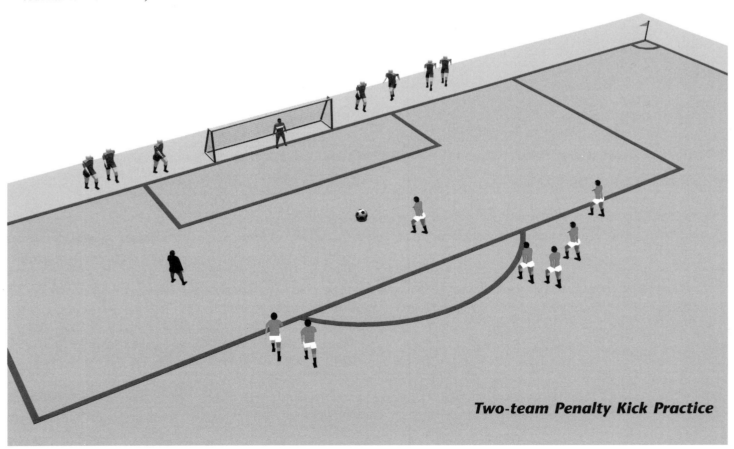

Two-team Penalty Kick Practice

At clinics I conduct for goalkeepers and coaches, I'm often asked what did I do on Penalties. So I tell them.

First of all I did my homework. I knew every regular penalty kicker in the First Division of the English League and kept a record of what they did — in my "little black book."

If a Penalty was conceded by our team — providing it wasn't given away by me! — I would relish the challenge of an almost "no-lose cover-yourself-in-glory" situation.

If I really knew the kicker's preference, I deliberately moved slightly off center of the goal and showed the kicker, marginally (hopefully almost imperceptibly), more space in the corner they normally kicked in. The law at that time did not allow the goalkeeper to move his or her feet until after the ball was kicked, but as the kicker moved towards the ball, I made a little fake move of the body to the "wrong side" — if I knew he'd shoot to his right, I'd fake a move to his left — and then launch myself to the right as the ball was kicked.

"What would happen?" coaches and goalkeepers would ask.

"They'd put it to my left!" I would joke.

Joking aside…it helped. It increased my chances of success. But I still picked most of the Penalties I faced from out of the back of the net. That's a fact of life for all goalkeepers!

But one Penalty saved can make the difference to a season. It can be the difference between winning or not winning a World Cup, a high school championship or a tournament. So anything that increases the percentage success rate should be considered.

You must practice Penalty Kicks!

The Shootout

This is an essential, if controversial, tie-breaker in playoff and tournament play. Therefore, it must be practiced.

In North America, the old NASL 35-yard Shootout tie-breaker is still used in some pro leagues. From a personal perspective, I feel it's a better way of deciding a game than by Penalty Kicks. It is a truer test of soccer skill — attacker-vs-goalkeeper. The Penalty Shootout is open to "cheating" by the keeper coming forward off the line before the kick is taken.

In my early days as coach of the Vancouver Whitecaps in the NASL, I didn't practice the Shootout. I wanted to go into games in a more positive frame of mind — that we were going to win the game in regulation time. Inevitably, it cost us — and reality and common sense began to kick in. So we started to practice the tie-breaking system after having been burned through lack of practice.

Apparently, Glen Hoddle, the England coach, fell into the same trap in the 1998 World Cup in France. Penalty Shootout practice was put on the back-burner. Argentina progressed into the Quarter-Finals at England's expense by their success in the tie-breaking phase — and through England's ineffectiveness in this situation.

No team can win every game. There will always be occasions when the score is tied at the end of regulation play and overtime. For sudden-death, tie-breaking tournament play, Penalty Shootouts must be practiced — and the practice can be fun!

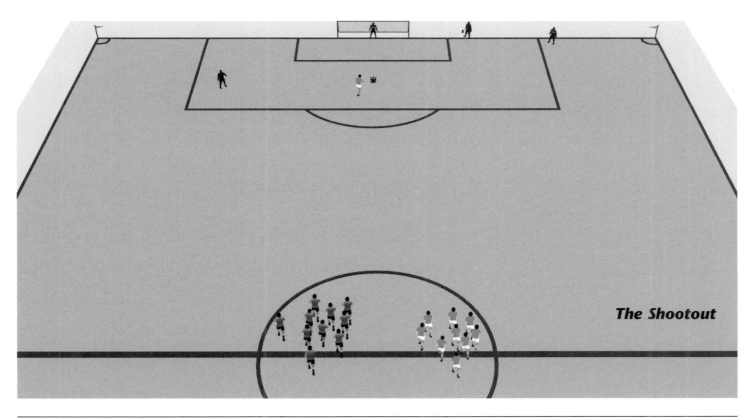

The Shootout

PELE AND PUSKAS

Not many goals are scored directly from a Kick-off, but that doesn't mean teams have to be complacent, especially goalkeepers.

The great Pele nearly scored from the Kick-off at the 1970 World Cup in Mexico (of course, we know the ball must first be passed forward by its own circumference). The ball went just over the cross bar with the goalkeeper beaten.

I nearly suffered a similar indignity in the mid-'60s, while playing with Blackpool. We were in a four-team tournament in Malaga, Spain. We were playing Real Madrid — the best club side in the world during the '60s.

Two Real Madrid players whose names will live forever in the annals of soccer legendary were Alfred Di Stefano and Ference Puskas. We'd had the audacity to score on them. We eventually lost 4-1!

On the Kick-off, I took up my usual position near the penalty spot when I saw Puskas looking up and down and muttering something to Di Stefano. The penny dropped just in time. I shuffled back as quickly as I could towards my goal while trying to keep on eye on what was happening. Di Stefano had tapped the kick to Puskas on his left side and Puskas had launched this incredible left-footed shot from the half-way line.

I just managed to catch the ball as it was going under the crossbar. If I'd have left it a split second longer, I may well have made it to the Guinness Book of Records — for the wrong reasons! How embarrassing that would have been!

Kick-offs, Goal Kicks & Dropped Balls

chapter 8

THE KICK-OFF STARTS IT ALL

Without the Kick-off, there is no game. It's the start of the game, the re-start after half-time and the re-start after a goal.

Most teams use the Kick-off merely to get a controlled possession in the Middle Third and take it from there.

Few goals are scored as a direct result of a Kick-off.

FINAL THIRD POSSESSION OR PRESSURE KICK-OFF

Some teams work on getting possession from the Kick-off in the Front Third — or at least pressure on the opposition in their Back Third — right from the Get-Go! It's not a bad idea. It sends out a clear signal — from Minute One or after being scored on — that you're organized and mean business (illustration on next page).

CONCENTRATING ON PLAYING DEAD

It's a fact, that the concentration of many players lapses when the game stops. Set Plays are often referred to as dead-ball situations. When the ball goes "dead" some players' minds go "dead." It's amazing how many players actually turn their backs on the ball as they retreat into defending positions.

This presents a great opportunity for the attacking team to take a quick, often short, Free Kick, Corner Kick or Throw-in with the defending team unprepared and taken by surprise (Triple A's). It's important for you, the coach, to remind players to be alert and alive at every stoppage to see what opportunities exist.

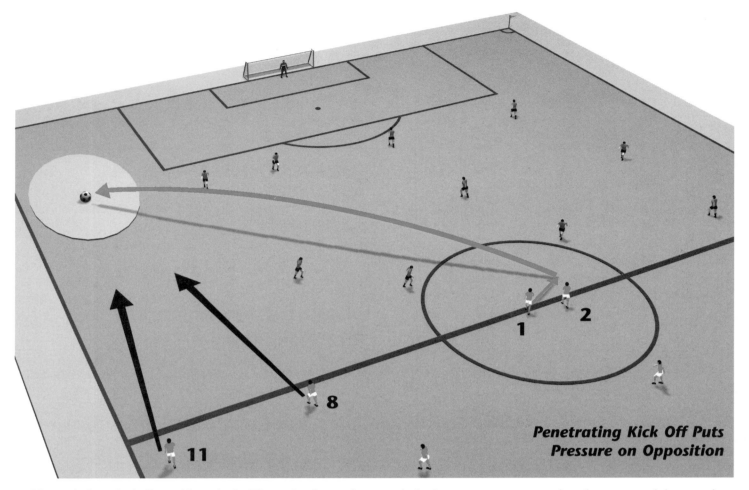

Penetrating Kick Off Puts Pressure on Opposition

Player 1 plays the ball considerately for **Player 2,** who sends a long diagonal ball over the top of the defenders into the area shown on the illustration. **Player 11** and **Player 8** race into that area either to gain possession — or to put pressure on the opponents and stop them playing out of their own end.

It helps if **Player 11** is a speed merchant (**Player 8,** too). As **Player 11** and **Player 8** go forward, they're supported by their teammates, who move up from the back to condense the space and to maintain the team shape.

In the old days on a Kick-off, before the no-handling back-pass rule for goalkeepers was introduced, teams would play the ball backwards and allow five or six players to touch the ball before finally playing it to the goalkeeper for his/her first handling touch — as a confidence booster. The keeper would usually kick long into the other half of the field.

Today, the back-pass rule has put that particular Set Play into the history books, but it's still worth considering a little possession soccer to pull the opposition forward and create more space behind them.

THE DROPPED BALL

The dropped ball is a Set Play that has little significance in soccer in terms of scoring or conceding goals — unlike its counterpart in hockey, the faceoff.

As both teams can get supporting players around the opposing one-on-one players on the Dropped Ball (there are no distance limitations for supporting players on either side at a dropped ball), it normally doesn't produce good controlled possession.

Dropped balls occur when a referee stops play with the ball still in the field of play — usually after what appears to be a serious injury that the referee wants to deal with as an emergency.

Rarely do we see Dropped Balls in scoring situations. It has the potential to produce a volatile situation. Referees normally use a little discretion in the hope of letting a clearance take place. On a Dropped Ball in front of the goal, the defending team is greatly disadvantaged — even though they have not committed an offense. So referees use the rule of common sense and don't give Dropped Balls in the penalty area — if they can avoid it.

Nevertheless, it is worth identifying a player on your team who is good in Dropped Ball situations.

THE GOAL KICK

For young players, the Goal Kick is a disadvantage rather than an advantage. It is difficult for, say, a nine year old to get any distance on the kick. That's one reason why young players under 12 should play a modified version of the game, where not only are the numbers reduced (3-a-side to 7-a-side, based on age), but so are the dimensions of the field.

Long Goal Kick Flicked-on by Striker

A "field" for a six year old should not be any longer than 30 yards. For a nine year old, no more than 50 yards.

At the higher levels of the game (14 years+), goalkeepers should be capable of "clearing their own lines," and should take Goal Kicks themselves. If they have to bring a defender back to take the Goal Kick, because of their own inabilities, it pulls a defender out of a better defending position and leaves the team unable to exploit and manipulate the offside rule.

No team should play "offside!" But every competitive 11-a-side team should take advantage and exploit the offside law to push opponents away from the goal. Even though opponents can't be offside on a goal kick, they will be if a ball is played to them after the initial kick.

The trick here is to estimate the distance a keeper can kick the ball from goal. Obviously, the longer a goalkeeper can kick with consistency, the more the back line can push up.

So goalkeepers are encouraged to take their own Goal Kicks — even if there is a back defender who is a better kicker than the keeper.

The defender who takes the Goal Kick and then runs out to join the line of defense has to work hard — both on the kick and the sprint to flatten out the line of defense. A poor kick from the normally good-kicking defender greatly exposes the defending team. Whereas, a not-so-good kick from the goalkeeper still has the defending team in good position and in good "shape" to deal with the problem.

So, wherever possible, goalkeepers should be encouraged, and helped in practice, to become better at taking Goal Kicks.

If the goalkeeper's good at it, and the strikers have good timing and heading ability, it's not unusual to create penetrating opportunities in the Front Third of the field (see the examples above and below).

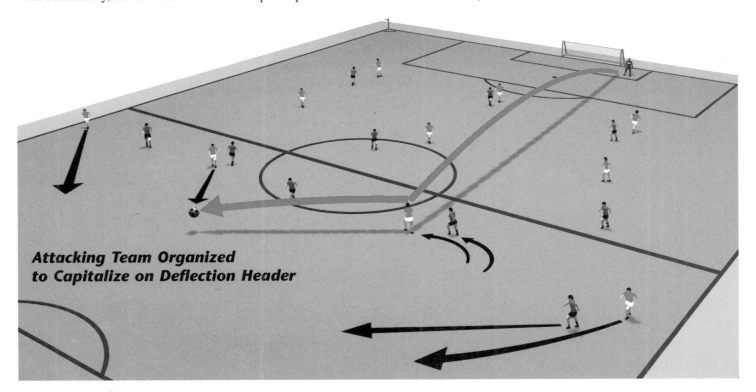

Attacking Team Organized to Capitalize on Deflection Header

Knowing a goalkeeper's distance and type of kick, a striker can push back on a defender, or go in behind if the defender refuses to be pushed back. The striker has to be able to time the run and judge the height of the ball, to move forward at the last second to flick-on a header in the direction of another striker or winger who times the run to gamble on a headed through ball and entry into the Back Third of the field.

Goalkeepers who lack length in their kick should look for a quick Goal Kick played wide — providing it is done with safety in mind. Young goalkeepers do have some real difficulty on Goal Kicks, and supporting field players should always help their keepers, by positioning for a short, usually wide, Goal Kick (see below).

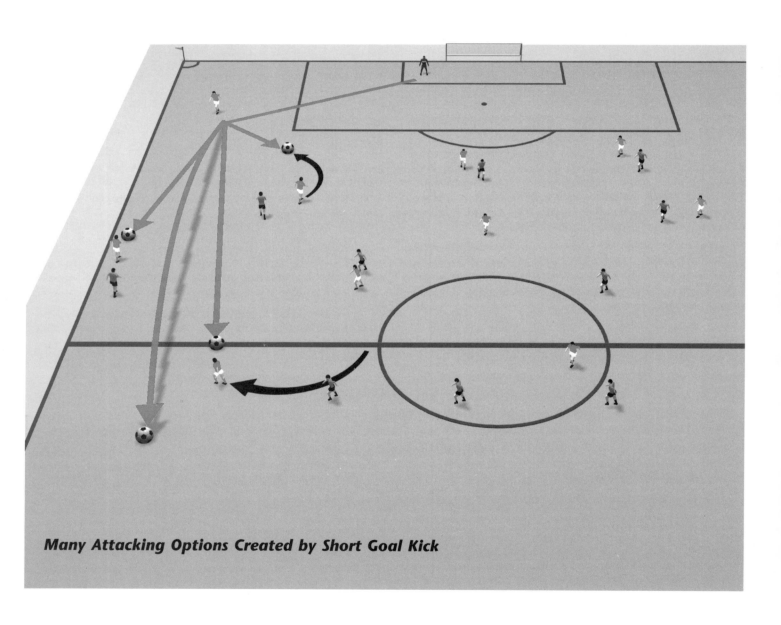

Many Attacking Options Created by Short Goal Kick

DEFENDING GOAL KICKS

It's important that teams pick up on the distance of an opposing goalkeeper's Goal Kicks as quickly as possible.

"Don't let it bounce!" is a good defending shout from the coach or a teammate as the ball is on its way.

The defending team needs to establish as early as possible — either in a game or from previous scouting information — the likely distance of the Goal Kick. Knowing that, the defending team establishes its line of defense — just above head height at the point the ball is coming down.

Allowing balls to bounce puts defenders back-footed, rather than flat-footed — stumbling back towards their own goal, unbalanced, trying to make contact with a disputed ball, with the odds greatly in favor of attackers who only need a little touch of the ball to create havoc.

Meeting the ball at the correct line of defense eliminates most of the problems, even if the player challenging for the ball fails in the initial challenge. By then, the supporting defenders have already fallen back into the correct supporting positions.

Even though the "punt" from the goalkeeper's hands is not a Set Play as such, the same thinking applies in establishing the line of defense. The maxim is: "Get your line of defense" distance right and then "don't let the ball bounce!"

So Goal Kicks, Kick-offs and Dropped Balls will not determine the outcome of a game to the same extent as Free Kicks, Corner Kicks and Penalties. Nevertheless, failure to attend to that detail (ATDs) could be costly. Be forewarned!

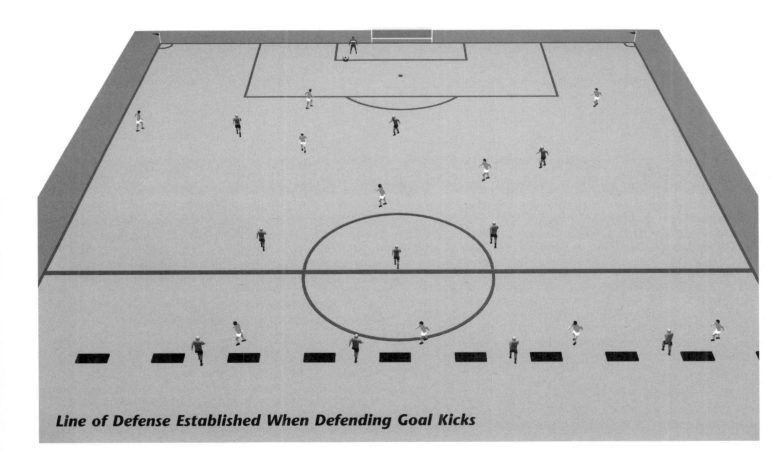

Line of Defense Established When Defending Goal Kicks

THE FULL MONTY!

The offside law may be the most important tactical law of soccer. If it's not, it is certainly the most controversial! Playing opponents "offside" catches up with you sooner or later.

In the '70s as Manager/Coach at Plymouth Argyle, when we were defending Free Kicks with our line of defense near the top of the box, we would execute "the Monty."

A split-second before the attacking Free Kick was taken, our back players would move out en-bloc to leave the less attentive attackers offside.

To trigger it, we decided to use "Monty" as the cue that we were going to use the trap. The name came from Monty Python — what else? — which was highly popular at that time. We had no Montys on the team, but you wouldn't know it when Bobby Saxton, our center back, called the play.

"Monty! Drop back a bit!" or "Monty!…" whatever Monty was required to do!

We'd deliberately set up our "line of defense" two or three yards closer to the goal than normal to invite the attackers to come in.

As you can imagine, there were risks involved, so we never took it for granted that offside would be called, even if we thought it was offside.

Our keeper, Jim Furnell, was instructed to be prepared to come "all the way" once the ball was played over the top of our defenders, whether he or our defense thought there were opponents offside or not. By the same rule, once our defenders moved up they would immediately recover towards the goal while appealing for the offside call, but never assuming the referee would give it. We would "play to the whistle."

We used the "Monty" more at home than we did on the road, obviously. Unlike the "Full Monty," we didn't want to get caught with our shorts down!

Overall, it was a great success and our fans loved it. The ploy worked. We looked as if we knew what we were doing. It gave the players a lot of satisfaction and pride.

Don't be tempted to do it too much, away from home. Now I'm not saying the referee and the assistant referees are "homers"…but also I'm not stupid!

THE INSWINGING '60s: HERE COMES BIG JACK

Many people think that the Inswinging Corner into the "Black Hole" area is an innovation of the '90s. Baaaahh! Wrong again! You need to go back to the Swinging '60s and Jack Charlton, who really introduced the Inswinging '60s.

It was Jack who popularized this great play while the resident center back at Leeds United. On most of Leeds' Attacking Corners, up would come Big Jack to place himself right in the eye of the "Black Hole" — four yards out from the goal line; one or two yards inside the line of the Near Post. Big Jack and his giraffe-type neck stood out as a landmark.

At Blackpool Football Club, in our wisdom or otherwise, we decided that our best bet would be to man-mark Jack. So our center forward, Ray Charnley — a great header of the ball, came back with Big Jack to make sure he was properly challenged. The outcome on our first effort was a goal for Leeds United. Not by Big Jack. Nor by any other Leeds player for that matter. It was a direct "gift" from me. As the Inswinging Corner Kick came in, I challenged for the ball, along with Ray and Big Jack. I had made the decision to punch the ball because of the heavy traffic. Just before punching the ball there was contact with my arm. It might have been Jack, but more likely it was Ray, my teammate. The ball skidded off my fist and into the net.

After that, our solution was no Ray Charnley marking Big Jack. It was up to me! It was my responsibility to take that area when the ball came in. Not the perfect solution — Big Jack was going to be effective in those situations no matter what marking system was used — but it was simple with one less body for me to worry about…and I knew what I had to do!

How to Teach & Coach Set Plays

No matter how good are your players, and how knowledgeable you and they are with regard to the game, unless you work on the execution of Set Plays, you have little chance.

Okay! Maybe you have a great Free Kick specialist or a smart player who single-handedly spots an opportunity and takes a quick shot at goal for a gift. If you have these people on your squad, encourage them. Normally it requires more than one or two players be "in on the act" for Set Plays to succeed. Defensively, it often needs the whole team to work together to deny the opposition.

Presented in the wrong way, Set Plays can be…boring! To have a team of 16 or more players standing around while you try to get it right is never going to be the most exciting thing in the world. Don't do any more of that than you have to (but you might have to do a little!)

The great reward, of course, is when a Set Play works…such as on a game-winning Free Kick. The players are usually prepared to stand around a bit longer at the next practice. But not much!

So the maxim for Set Plays is "little but often" while using whatever method you can to reinforce the detail. Little reminders here, there and everywhere. Well, almost! You don't want the opposition to be in on the act, too!

Weather plays a critical part. Trying to get the detail worked out on the practice field with the temperature at 35°F and the rain bucketing down will be more difficult than in a balmy 73 degrees. Always, there must be a sense of occasion.

Remember what we said in the Introduction, that 25% or more of all goals are the result of Set Plays and, on the basis of that, you should spend 25% or more of your "team play" preparation time on Set Plays. It's a good idea to record the amount of time you use. It goes without saying that other aspects of team preparation can't be neglected. What's the point of being great at Attacking Corners and Attacking Free Kicks in the Final Front if you never get into the opposition's half?

SQUARE PEGS SKILLS COMPETITION

If you've been coaching your players for some time, you'll have a good idea of who can do what, but it's not always that obvious.

It is essential you utilize your players in their most effective positions. Who can inswing the best ball from the right corner and left corner? Who has the strongest and most accurate shot at goal from 25 yards?

Who can bend the ball around or over the wall and just under the crossbar, and inside the post furthest away from the keeper? Who can flick-on the ball best at the Near Post from a corner into the Black Hole?

Rotation Corner Kick Flick-on Competition

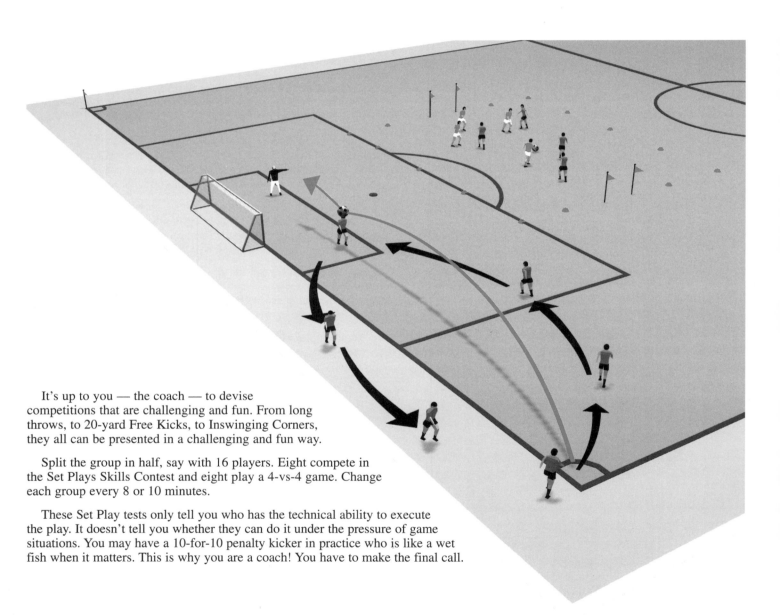

It's up to you — the coach — to devise competitions that are challenging and fun. From long throws, to 20-yard Free Kicks, to Inswinging Corners, they all can be presented in a challenging and fun way.

Split the group in half, say with 16 players. Eight compete in the Set Plays Skills Contest and eight play a 4-vs-4 game. Change each group every 8 or 10 minutes.

These Set Play tests only tell you who has the technical ability to execute the play. It doesn't tell you whether they can do it under the pressure of game situations. You may have a 10-for-10 penalty kicker in practice who is like a wet fish when it matters. This is why you are a coach! You have to make the final call.

Small-Group Set Play Practice

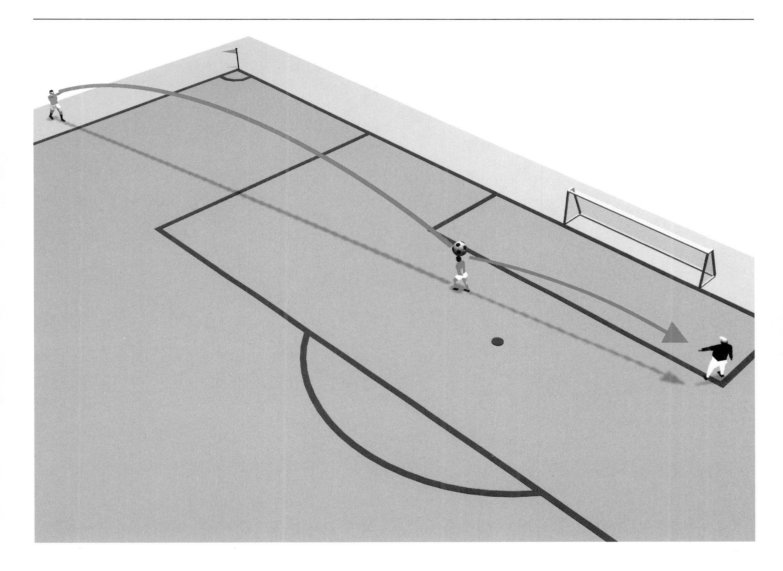

It's often possible to work in small groups for Set Play practice just using the principal players involved in the Set Play. Do this before, during or after practice.

For instance, if you wanted to practice a long throw and a flick-on in the Near Post area, you only need two players for that part of the play — with a coach or assistant coach perhaps positioned in the Far Post area as the target for the flick-on.

Similarly, with Attacking Throw-ins and Attacking Free Kicks, the one, two, three, or four players who execute the principal part of the play can spend productive time getting their part — the major part — of the Set Play perfected.

Shadow Play

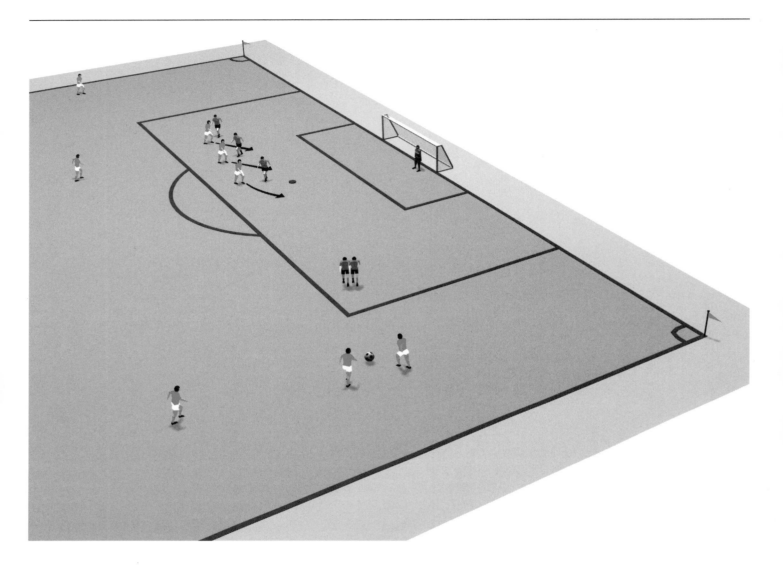

Playing 11-vs-1 or 11-vs-5 (or 6) is always a good idea to help the team develop the patterns of play and to gain an understanding of teammates' likes and dislikes, abilities and inabilities.

We've devoted a whole chapter to Shadow Play in the manual "Coaching the Team," which is a part of this "Coaching Series." If you want to study the method in more detail, refer to that chapter in the book.

The great advantage of Shadow Play is that the coach can easily call the play: "Free Kick on the edge of the box" as play arrives just outside the penalty area. Or: "Attacking Corner Kick!" or "Defending Corner!"

With normal teams of 15 to 18 players, it's easy to set up the situations required.

The short-handed group of five or six players become the wall and space markers on a Free Kick. The coach and assistant coach can join in to swell the short-handed numbers.

Shadow Play is not one of soccer's most favorite practice methods. But it works. So here again, the discretion of the coach is used to determine just how long you're going to work on this. You are well-advised to keep the Shadow Play moving as much as possible and encourage and inspire players for that extra bit of effort and concentration.

11-vs-11 Play

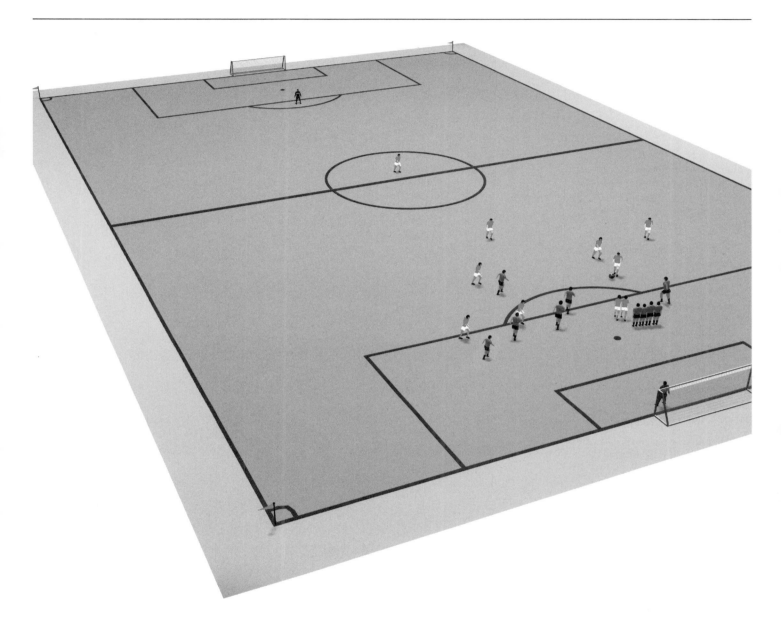

Two teams of 11 on a regulation field gives you the nearest thing to game conditions. If you have a squad of 22, you're lucky (or unlucky, depending on the way you look at it!) as you can easily — and on your own terms — work for 20 or 25 minutes in Set Play situations in an 11-vs-11 game.

If you want to work on a particular play — e.g., Attacking Free Kick, centrally, 22 yards from goal — you just blow the whistle and award the Free Kick.

Or better still, make them work for the privilege. "You need to get eight consecutive passes and with the last three in the attacking half to win the Free Kick."

If you don't have 22 players, think about arranging a practice game with another local team, and for 20 or 30 minutes condition the game so that goals can only be scored from Set Plays. Use the eight-consecutive-pass rule to win Corners, Free Kicks, etc.

11-vs-11 Possession

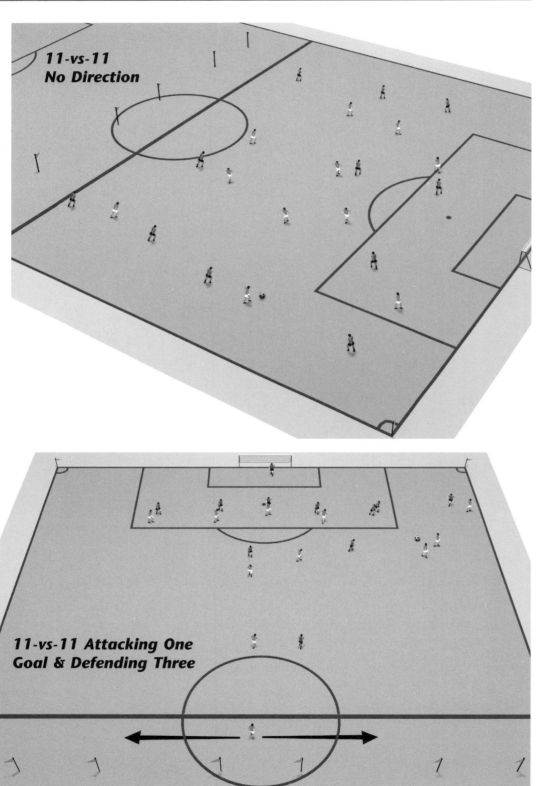

**11-vs-11
No Direction**

**11-vs-11 Attacking One
Goal & Defending Three**

Start with 11-vs-11 possession play in a half field with no direction or offside. The team that makes 4 (or 5 or 6) consecutive passes wins the Attacking Corner (Free Kick, Throw-in).

From the Attacking Set Play, in this case a Free Kick, all the normal 11-a-side rules apply — direction, goal, offside — until the play is either finished successfully or repelled by the defending team, or the ball is out of play. Three target goals are put up just inside the other half of the field for the defenders to play out to if they gain possession after defending a Set Play. They must shoot from inside their defending half.

The goalkeeper of the attacking team stays in the other half of the field and is required to defend all three goals (and can use his or her hands).

At the end of a particular phase, the coach re-starts the possession game with a Dropped Ball.

One point is awarded for a "halfway goal" by the defending side. Four points for the "perfect" Set Play goal. Two points for "seconds" or "gifts."

The War Game

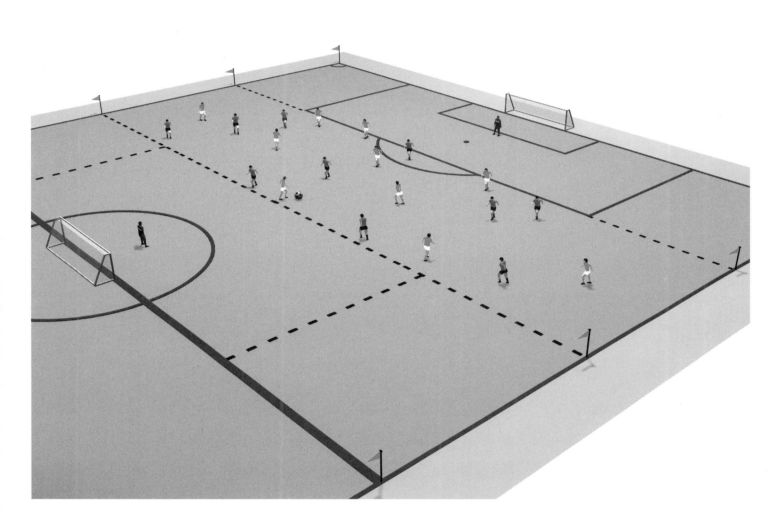

Set up a portable goal at the half-way line. Mark in with paint or marker disks a Penalty Box from the half-way line.

Play 11-vs-11 on half-field with offside only in the final third of the reduced field (i.e., an extension of the 18-yard-line).

Four or five consecutive passes produces the designated Set Play (e.g., Free Kick, Attacking Corner, etc.).

Regular-play goals score one; Set Play goals score four. This keeps the game challenging and fun.

Game is restarted after a goal by a dropped ball at midfield.

9-vs-9 Possession

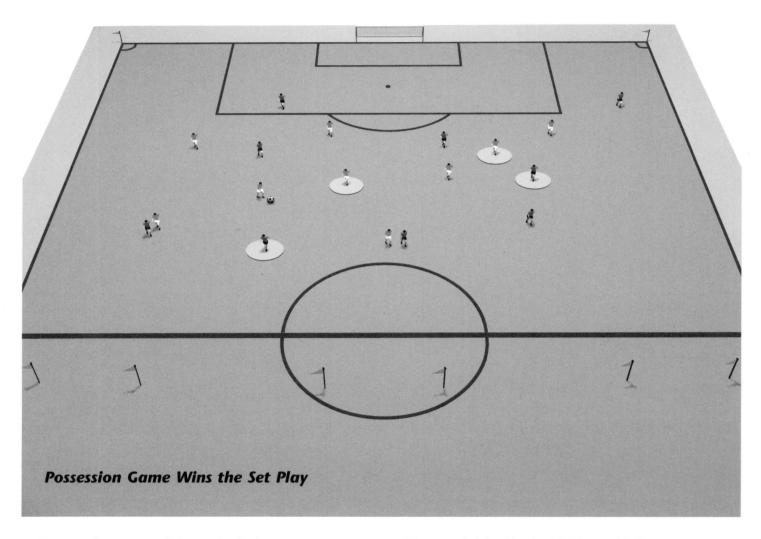

Possession Game Wins the Set Play

There are four groups of players, in pinnies:

7 Reds (including a goalkeeper) combine with 2 Whites

7 Blues (including a goalkeeper) combine with 2 Greens.

The "White" and "Green" players are shown within the four white circles. Possession game in half-field — no direction, no goals (above). The first team to get five consecutive passes is awarded the designated Set Play (Free Kick, Corner, etc.).

That team is joined by the 2 Whites and 2 Greens (next page) to make an attacking team of 11. The attacking team goalkeeper goes into the other half of the field to defend the three goals, as in 11-vs-11 possession.

You will likely have to juggle the numbers as most squads are not 18 strong. Coaches and assistant coaches or trainers can be added for the Set Play phase.

Continued on next page

For the Set Play, the action is still restricted to the half of the field, except for the three-goal goalkeeper. The normal 11-a-side rules of play (including offside) for the Set Play phase, which finishes after a successful play, or when the ball goes out of play or when the short-handed team clears the ball (or the team defending the Set Play scores a goal through one of the three goals in the other half of the field). Restart with a dropped ball.

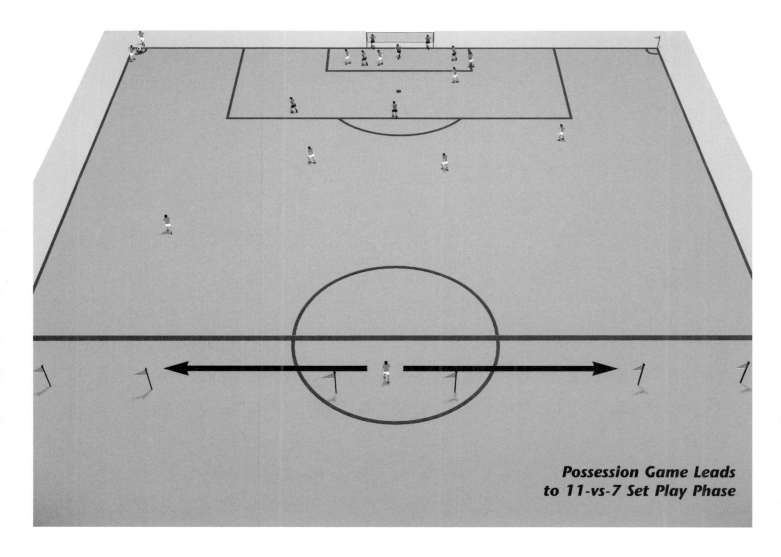

Possession Game Leads to 11-vs-7 Set Play Phase

8-vs-8 Mini War Game

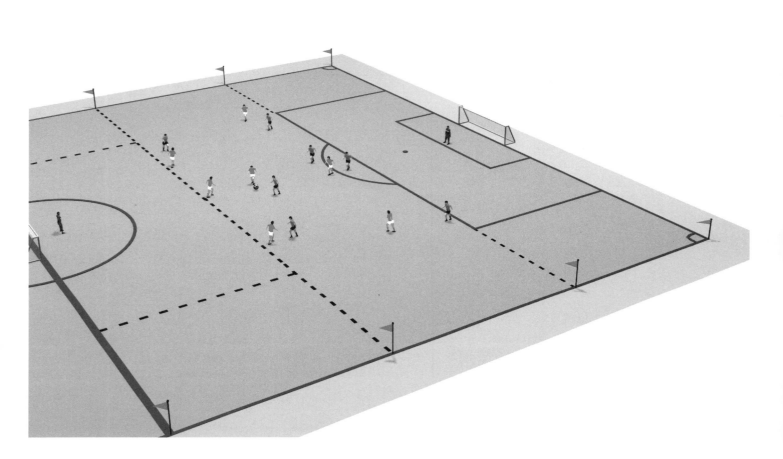

An 8-vs-8 (or 7-vs-7, 9-vs-9) version, with a goal on half-way line, employs the same rules as the 11-vs-11 half-field version. Five – or three or four – consecutive passes wins the designated Set Play (Corner, Free Kick or Throw-in).

There is no adjustment of numbers in awarding the Set Play. It remains 8-vs-8.

While this is limiting in terms of the team preparation (11 players), it gives repeated opportunities for Set Plays with most of the elements of 11-a-side re-starts.

Off The Field

The "little and often" maxim continues off the field:

1. The Team Meeting

The "chalk talk" is another opportunity to spell out roles and responsibilities visually.

2. Video Analysis

Looking at video of your own team and of other teams is a captivating way of reinforcing the methods to be used — or not used — by your own team.

3. The Locker Room Wall

Last-minute reminders on the locker room wall should only be that — reminders. If they don't know their roles by now, you're in trouble. Encourage the substitutes to study all the requirements and the personnel they could be replacing (see the photo). At the back of the book are templates to copy for the locker room wall (pages 98, 99 & 100).

4. High-tech Help

Today's high-tech world is producing more and more powerful learning systems where three-dimensional software graphically shows who does what, when and where on Set Plays (see the video that accompanies this book).

5. Sweet Dreams

Trevor Hartley, the former West Ham United player and Tottenham Hotspurs, Luton Town and Sunderland coach — and national coach for Malaysia, had a neat way of reinforcing the Set Plays the night before a game when his teams were on the road. Just before curfew, he would roam the hotel corridors posting the Set Play sheets under each player's door. He reasoned that a clear reminder just before going to sleep would effectively lodge in their minds what their roles were on Set Plays.

AN OLD PLOY BY AN OLD KEEPER

As a goalkeeper, my kicking off the ground wasn't so great — no matter how much I practiced. From my hands I had no difficulties. So this is what we would do.

My wide fullback, on the side from which the Goal Kick was to be taken, would begin to walk towards the half-way line as if we were taking a conventional (long) Goal Kick.

Naturally, the opposition's winger on that side would go with him.

The difference was our fullback would walk on the outside of the marker — the "wrong side" — and when the winger looked back or to the inside of the field, my fullback would sprint back towards the outside of the penalty area from the "blindside" of their winger.

I would play a short Goal Kick, the fullback would pass it back to me and I would have the ball in my hands at the top of the box.

It worked almost every time. Great! Except that with today's back-pass rule, the ball can't be picked up by the keeper.

Oh well! I don't think I'll be playing for England again. Or for anyone else of consequence, for that matter!

A FUNNY THING HAPPENED ON THE WAY TO KING GEORGE V PLAYING FIELD

September 1985.

A tie or a win against Honduras in St. John's, Newfoundland, would give Canada its first-ever appearance in a World Cup Final. However, Canada was hurting because of injuries and suspensions.

English-born Carl Valentine, who had become a Canadian citizen while with the Vancouver Whitecaps of the old NASL, was playing for West Bromich Albion in England. Carl had declined to play for the Canadian National team in the 1984 Olympics, because he still had ambitions of playing for England, which as a dual citizen he was eligible to do

One year later, we persuaded Carl that he had a better chance of being selected for Canada in the World Cup than for England. With only one game to go for qualification, he could make a dream come true — for him and for us!

We changed our preparation plans especially to accommodate Carl. Instead of assembling in St. John's early in the week, we met instead in Toronto, the Monday preceding the Saturday game.

On Tuesday night, we played a game against London Marconi, a very good semi-pro team, to get the team shape worked out and to fit Carl into the patterns of play. Unfortunately, Carl had been sick the night before — too much travel, excitement and expectations — and we could only afford to play him for half a game, but that was more than helpful.

We set aside the next day, Wednesday, to go to a remote soccer park outside of Toronto to practice our Set Plays and in particular, our Attacking Corners. Carl was to be our Corner Kicker from the left (Carl, a right winger, with a great right foot. Inswinging Corners. Square Pegs!).

Foiled again! CBC Television came out to do a "special" for a pre-game program. With cameras whirring for our 75-minute session, we weren't going to give anything away. There were no Set Plays!

Arriving at St. John's on Thursday, we did two critically important things.

The coaching staff immediately took a cab to inspect the King George V Stadium, where the game was being played on Saturday. A running track around the outside of the field cut across the very extremity of each Corner. It forced the Corner Kicker to step up six inches to place the non-kicking foot in position to take the kick — making it difficult. I had a word with the groundskeeper and we built four sand runways at each of the four Corners.

Then, through our CSA board member in Newfoundland, George Innes, we found a private school with a totally enclosed soccer field. Early Friday morning, we left the hotel by bus for the school. We spent 75 minutes working on our Corners and Free Kicks, and then jumped back on the bus to go to King George V field for the "official" open practice — with media from Canada and Honduras in attendance. A couple of reporters remarked after that they were somewhat surprised about such a light workout before such an important game. Little did they know!

The next day, we beat Honduras 2-1 to take Canada to its first and so far, only appearance in the Men's World Cup Final. Both Canada goals came from Corner Kicks taken by...Carl Valentine!

Footnote: I returned to St. John's, Newfoundland, six years after the historic day for Canadian soccer. I was the guest at the Canadian men's club finals — at King George V Stadium. The sand runways at the corner of the soccer field on the no-longer used track were still there — and were now covered with sparse grass.

Appendix

SCOUTING THE OPPOSITION

It goes without saying that the more you know about your opponents — their strengths and the weaknesses — the better your chance of success on Set Plays. Who is the Free Kick specialist? What does he or she do? Do they have a Long Throw specialist? Are they well-organized defensively on Free Kicks? Do they man-mark or zone-mark on Corner Kicks? Who is their penalty kicker and where does he or she prefer to place the ball? What do they do on Attacking Corners?

The audit goes on!

Whether scouting the opposition yourself or you are have someone else do it, make sure you find out the other team's weaknesses on Set Plays, so you can exploit them.

TAKE WHAT YOU'RE GIVEN

Ron Moran and I were co-coaching youth players at Liverpool Football Club in the early '70s. We had spent part of the week working on a new Free Kick.

On the Saturday, we played at Blackpool and were awarded a direct Free Kick in the perfect position. When the ball was put down the Blackpool team was in complete disarray — no wall, goalkeeper on the post trying to organize. It was an empty-net shot.

"Floody! Floody!"

Ron and I were screaming from 50 yards away at Eddie Flood, our "organizer" of Free Kicks.

"Okay! Know what to do!" waved Eddie.

Blackpool got organized. Our Free Kick didn't work. No goal.

After the game, Ron Moran was still upset

"Floody! Why didn't you kick it in the empty net?"

"Well, I was waiting for us to get organized for our planned Free Kick."

"Take what you're given, young man. Don't let Tony and me steal your brains!" was the somewhat aggressive, and sound, advice from Ron.

INDIRECT FREE KICKS

Indirect Free Kick Less Than 10 Yards from Goal

Indirect Free Kicks inside the penalty area are a hassle — particularly for the referee. So referees tend to use a little discretion and stay away from them if they can. But they do happen occasionally and, as coach, you should be prepared — both from an attacking and defensive perspective.

What should you do defensively about Indirect Free Kicks within the penalty area? Here are two ways of dealing with the Indirect Free Kick from a defensive viewpoint, but first it goes without saying that every single person comes back to help. This is a very dangerous situation.

FREE KICKS LESS THAN 10 YARDS FROM GOAL

If it's closer to the goal than 10 yards, everyone is lined up across the goal line — tallest on the outside, shortest in the middle — with the goalkeeper covering the center (the rule is 10 yards from the ball on a Free Kick, but you're allowed to stay in the field of play) as we show in the illustration above.

Everyone back.

Split wall into 5+5 with tallest players on the outside.

The goalkeeper needs to have a clear view of the ball, but should be slightly in front of the wall to enable the keeper to defend as much of the goal as possible. It may mean that the 10 players in the wall are slightly behind the goal line with the keeper forward of them with his or her heels on the goal line.

As the angle is a widened off-center, the wall-split needs to be adjusted to allow the keeper to be more effectively positioned. For instance, the wall may be 4+6 wall or a 3+7 or 2+5 wall — depending on the angle.

Even though the shot is indirect, some teams take a mighty direct shot at the wall to look for a deflection into goal off a defender. So the wall must remain resolute.

In most cases the attacking team will "work" a Free Kick and play the ball to a teammate for the shot. This gives a split-second for the keeper to move out a yard or so to narrow the

*Indirect Free Kick
Just Inside the Penalty Area*

angle. The rest of the team can do the same, but it's better to stay solid and determined (and brave!).

FREE KICK JUST INSIDE THE PENALTY AREA

Everyone back.

From this angle, split wall into 3+5, with tallest players on the outside.

Goalkeeper with clear view of the ball, but behind the line of the wall (to prevent the chip shot). Two "Bullet Men" come in from right and left to put as much pressure on the strikers as possible (it's an Indirect Free Kick so the ball must be played by more than one player for a goal to count).

From an attacking perspective, you probably don't want to roll the ball forward as this will close the angle. Sideways, or maybe a little backwards, gives more time and space to make a shot. A driven ball? A toe poke close to goal? Aim for the top corner?

The short pass to the side for the trapping of the ball by a teammate gives a dead-ball opportunity for the shooter (we've suggested that play both on short corners and at Free Kicks outside the box). But that takes a fraction of a second longer than shooting the moving ball.

You might want to practice the situation to see who are your best players at executing. Even though this situation may only happen once in a season, one goal can make a huge difference.

THE AGE OF SET PLAYS

Set Plays are part of soccer from Day One. How can you start a game without a Set Play? How do you re-start a game after the ball has gone out of play...or after a stoppage...or after a goal has been scored?

Of course, awarding a Penalty Kick is ridiculous for players of age 6 or 7. When a "major" offense such as a hand ball or a trip occurs near the goal, it should be quickly explained why this is incorrect — why it's a "foul" — and the game should be re-started with an indirect Free Kick. These young players, generally, make honest errors and do not commit malicious fouls. They should be educated, not punished.

It's only as players begin to enter more formal soccer — at age 9 and 10 — that the full implications and range of Set Plays becomes necessary. Offside produces a Free Kick, but what 7 or 8 year old needs to be concerned about offside?

As children approach 12 or 13, they should know all the ins and outs of situations that produce a Set Play — Kick-offs, Corner Kicks, Penalties, Direct and Indirect Free Kicks — the reasons why and the laws that accompany them.

From 14 years and up, the tactics and strategies surrounding Set Plays become increasingly important. That's what this book is about. However, it would be a shame if your U-18 team failed to take advantage of a Throw-in in the Attacking Third of the field, when trailing 1-0 in a championship game with five minutes to go, because the ball was thrown incorrectly and therefore given back to the opposition. This is a skill that should be learned at age 6.

Modifying the game, the field and goal sizes to make sure the game — and the rules — fit the child is the best way for children to grow with the game and to develop an understanding of Set Plays and how to explore or counter them.

Our own Total Player Development™ Program uses a progressive development in games, skills and rules — from our One-with-One™ program for 4 and 5 year olds moving into 11-vs-11 at age 12 and 13.

AGE 4 & 5

KICK-OFF
Learn how to kick the ball.
GOAL KICK
Can be used, but not important.
THROW-IN
Introduction to Throw-in in One-with-One™.
FREE KICK
Not Applicable
OFFSIDE FREE KICK
Not Applicable
CORNER KICK
Not Applicable
PENALTY
Not Applicable
DROPPED BALL
Not Applicable

AGE 6 & 7

KICK-OFF
Rudimentary introduction in modified and 3-vs-3 Micro Soccer™.
GOAL KICK
Important Set Play for modified and 3-vs-3 Micro Soccer™.
THROW-IN
Great age to learn this technique — once and for all!
FREE KICK
Only as a learning opportunity, e.g., after a blatant handball (indirect).

OFFSIDE FREE KICK
Not Applicable
CORNER KICK
Explain what a Corner Kick is and how to take it.
PENALTY
Not Applicable – Indirect Free Kick instead and explanation.
DROPPED BALL
Not Applicable

AGE 8 & 9

KICK-OFF
To start and re-start the game (after a goal).
GOAL KICK
Longer Goal Kicks on slightly bigger field (4 vs 4).
THROW-IN
Longer throws for distance. Technique developed.
FREE KICK
Gradual progression into what is legal and illegal — indirect.
OFFSIDE FREE KICK
Not Applicable
CORNER KICK
Modified field to make sure the Corner Kick is possible into center goal area. Elements of how to defend on Corners. Blindside runs in attacking.
PENALTY
Not Applicable
Indirect Free Kick instead.
DROPPED BALL
Shown and practiced.

AGE 10 & 11

KICK-OFF

Mini Soccer and 7-vs-7 soccer on a scaled-down field with Kick-off.

GOAL KICK

Playing Goal Kick wide and away from danger.

THROW-IN

Some aspects of going away — and leaving space for receiving the ball.

FREE KICK

Potentially dangerous inclination to use best kicker on attack (understandable). Start of defensive organization.

OFFSIDE FREE KICK

Introduction to the offside rule. Applied in Mini Soccer and 7-vs-7 soccer on scaled-down field.

CORNER KICK

Modified field to make sure the Corner Kick is possible into center goal area. Short Corner on attack. Elements of how to defend Corners.

PENALTY

Introduction of Penalty and reasons why.

DROPPED BALL

Little importance.

AGE 12 & 13

KICK-OFF

FIFA rules for the Kick-off.

GOAL KICK

Fields may be too big. Wide Goal Kicks — maybe by a defender.

THROW-IN

Simple tactical throws.

FREE KICK

Potentially dangerous inclination to use best kicker on attack (understandable). Start of defensive organization.

OFFSIDE FREE KICK

FIFA application of the Offside Law.

CORNER KICK

Modified (smaller) field to make sure the Corner Kick is possible into center goal area. Elements of how to defend Corner Kicks. Short Corner and Pull Back.

PENALTY

FIFA rules.

DROPPED BALL

Little importance.

AGE 14-16

KICK-OFF

FIFA rules on Kick-off with some elements of tactical plays.

GOAL KICK

Goalkeeper encouraged to take own Goal Kicks.

THROW-IN

Throwing through the thirds of the field.

FREE KICK

Tactical understanding of direct vs indirect. Understanding of Free Kicks through the thirds. Defensive organization practice.

OFFSIDE FREE KICK

FIFA application of the Offside Law, and its tactical implications.

CORNER KICK

Tactical Corner Kicks — particularly Short and Pull Back.

PENALTY

Regular practice on Penalties (tournament/tie breaker).

DROPPED BALL

Little importance.

AGE 17-plus

KICK-OFF

FIFA rules on Kick-off with some elements of tactical plays.

GOAL KICK

Continuous work on distance kicking, as an essential way to relieve territorial pressure.

THROW-IN

Attacking and Defending Throw-ins — particularly in Final Third. "Down-the-line" understanding.

FREE KICK

Up there with Corner Kicks in terms of importance and team understanding. Needs constant practice/reinforcement.

OFFSIDE FREE KICK

FIFA application of the Offside Law, and its tactical implications.

CORNER KICK

After the Penalty, the most important Set Play. Attacking and defending need complete team understanding and cooperation. Inswinging and Outswinging Corners, Short Corners and Pull Backs.

PENALTY

Important Set Play that will win or lose games and decide (tie breakers) tournament games.

DROPPED BALL

Little importance.

THE AMERICAN THROW

The '90s brought the spectacular American Throw to soccer fields of the world — produced by a handspring starting from a standing position 5 or 6 yards from the touchline.

With both hands on the ball and the ball taking the place of the hands in a conventional handspring, in effect, it becomes a "ballspring." The momentum helps develop the power and velocity to throw the ball long distances, sometimes approaching 50 yards — the Far Post in the Attacking Third.

The throw is a remarkable piece of athleticism but is in declining use today because it's difficult to produce consistency of length and accuracy.

Planned throws need consistent execution. Corner Kicks and Free Kicks should be aimed at certain spaces that the potential scorers know they must arrive at the same time as the ball.

In that regard, the conventional Long Throw produces fewer "Oohs" and "Aahs" — but more goals.

This Bud's for You!

This is not a lament for the passing of the wing forward position — "wingers" as they were fondly called. There are still some around today and the game will always use the wide areas of the field to build successful attacking play.

What this is, however, is a story about a great soccer character, Willie Johnston. Willie is the former Glasgow Rangers, West Bromich Albion, Vancouver Whitecaps and Scotland left winger. And for those that did not know Willie as a player, this is to let you know just what you missed.

If goalkeepers are crazy, then wingers are only a brain cell or two behind. Let's just call them unpredictable — and nearly always mercurial!

Willie entered soccer's Hall of Shame when he tested positive at the 1978 World Cup in Argentina. He was sent home — banned from any further play. The "drug" that Willie took — passed on to him by another player — was to help settle him in readiness to play. It was equivalent in strength to four cups of coffee. Had you been in the locker room before a game you'd have seen why Willie was tempted into the soccer "fix." He was so nervous, so on edge, you would think he might explode. All because he so badly wanted to do well on the field.

Once there, he was all you wanted a winger to be (unless you were his coach!).

He was a great dribbler, an entertainer and had explosive speed over 5 or 6 yards. He was a joker, a fighter and a great crosser. Terrific to watch. Difficult to coach, of course! But worth it. Yes! Yes! Yes!

When first introduced to a large gathering of Vancouver media in 1979 (the year after Argentina), his reputation had obviously preceded him. As the Whitecaps coach, I told the media that Willie had chosen Vancouver because it was the drug capital of Canada. They laughed and that was the end of it. He was left to get on with his soccer entertainment. And entertain he did.

Willie is still revered in Vancouver today for his exploits on the field. In those days, all the Whitecaps away games were carried live by BCTV.

One June night, at Spartan Stadium in San Jose, the Whitecaps were playing the Earthquakes, and the score was tied at 1 - 1 with five minutes to go. We were down to 10 men. Roger Kenyon had committed some trivial indiscretion (as I recall!!) and had been dispatched to the locker room for "an early bath." We won a corner on the right side and Willie made his way over as part of the team plan (Inswinging Corner with his great left foot). As he approached the corner flag in the tight San Jose stadium, a fan leaned over the wall and offered him a drink from his can of Budweiser. Willie took a swig, put the ball down, crossed the corner...and Peter Daniels came in for the inch-perfect cross to head the winning goal.

That incident got so many replays on BCTV it was stuck indelibly in the memory of every Whitecaps' fan.

Ten years later, at the reunion game in Vancouver to celebrate the winning of the Soccer Bowl by the Whitecaps in 1979, the first corner of the night from the right side found Willie coming over to take it. But before he could kick the ball, up stepped a waiter in black tie and tails with a Budweiser on a silver platter for Willie to have his gulp.

Coincidentally, Willie's nickname is Bud. "So: Willie...This Bud's for you!"

Direct or Indirect?

According to Law 12, a Direct Free Kick is awarded to the opposing team if a player commits an offense that is adjudged by the Referee to be careless, reckless or uses excessive force. Among the offenses that fall into that category are kicking, striking, tripping, pushing and holding. So does deliberately handling the ball (other than the goalkeeper in his/her own penalty area).

The Direct Free Kick is taken from the place where the offense occurred and the ball can be scored with one kick into the goal. If a "direct" free kick offense occurs in the penalty area, a Penalty Kick is awarded.

An Indirect Free Kick is awarded if, in the opinion of the Referee, a player commits one of the three following offenses:
1. Plays in a dangerous manner.
2. Impedes the progress of an opponent (obstruction).
3. Prevents the goalkeeper from releasing the ball from his/her hands.

A goalkeeper can concede an Indirect Free Kick by:
• Taking more than four steps while controlling the ball with the hands before releasing it.
• Picking the ball up after having already had it in the hands before putting it down.
• Touching the ball with the hands after it has been deliberately played to the keeper by one of his/her teammates.
• Touching the ball with the hands after it has been thrown in to the keeper by a teammate.
• Deliberately wasting time.

In the goalkeeper incidents, the Free Kicks occur mostly in the penalty box and produce a difficult situation for the defending team (see the Appendix, page 86 & 87).

It is critical for a player taking a Free Kick to know whether it's a Direct or an Indirect Free Kick. What a disappointment it would be, not to mention embarrassment, to score a magnificent one-shot goal only to see the Referee award a Goal Kick to the opposition because it was an Indirect Free Kick and only one player had touched the ball!

The Referee should clearly indicate an Indirect Free Kick by raising his arm above his head and maintaining his arm in that position until the kick has been taken and the ball has touched another player or the ball goes out of play.

For a goal to count on an Indirect Free Kick, at least two players must have touched the ball before it enters the net. The "other player" does not have to be a teammate. That's why, on an Indirect Free Kick in the penalty area 10 yards or less from the goal, an attacker may take an almighty whack at the ball with the intention of striking an opponent in the wall standing on the goal line in the hope of getting a deflection into the goal.

If in doubt, it's worth a player having a quiet word with the Referee!

"Of course it's direct," the Ref might say. "I haven't put my arm up, have I? Don't you know the rules of the game?"

Better admonishment than disappointment and embarrassment.

And that's why a goalkeeper who knows the kick is indirect may deliberately let a direct kick enter the net without making any effort to stop the ball. Brave goalkeeper!

So takers of Free Kicks must make sure they know what type of kick it is. And goalkeepers, be careful out there!

KEEP IT SIMPLE

When the now legendary manager/coach of Liverpool, Bill Shankly, arrived at Anfield Road from Huddersfield Town in the '60s , the Mighty Reds were languishing in the Second Division. Their arch-rivals, Everton — the other Merseyside club — were prospering in the First Division. The first task for Shanks was to improve morale and confidence.

On the practice field, he did two simple things:

1. He played 3-a-side soccer with teams made up of players who frequently played together in the 11-a-side game. Right fullback, right winger, right midfielder as one team; striker, left winger, left midfielder as another. He produced triangles of confidence and competence.

2. The second thing was to introduce a simple Throw-in. If the thrower was unmarked, the ball was thrown to the outside foot of an incoming player who side-foot volleyed it back to the thrower to gain a controlled possession. Liverpool still uses the throw today.

I guess that further reinforces the KISS principle ("Keep It Simple, Stupid").

THE WALLMEN AND THE BULLET MAN

On Free Kicks around the penalty area, nobody in their right mind enjoys the "privilege" of being in the wall, or being the "Bullet Man." They are both lousy jobs...but somebody has got to do them!

We've discussed how members of the wall can be more effective elsewhere in this book.

The Bullet Man has to be a special individual as he or she has to — or should! — put everything on the line for the team. It is on Indirect Free Kicks or when a team plays a short pass to open up the angle at a Direct Free Kick that the Bullet Man has to be at his or her best. As soon as the ball is played, the Bullet Man attempts to charge the ball to block the shot on goal.

As I've already said, my preference as a team coach and a former goalkeeper is to have the Bullet Man attacking from a slight angle — rather than from straight on. This allows the Bullet Man to stretch out the nearest foot/leg to block the shot, but just as importantly, it allows the goalkeeper to have a clear view of the ball, and still be able to deal with a deflection if the Bullet Man makes a partial block. The angle of approach is also a little less intimidating for the Bullet Man (see page 50).

GLOSSARY OF TERMS

Bullet Man
A defending player near to a free kick who attempts to charge down a shot at goal

Dead Balls
Another term used to describe Set Plays.

Far Post
Usually the area in front of the far post rather than the post itself. Offside rule plays a big part as to how far out the Far Post area will be.

The Mixer
An expression to describe the area right in front of the goal in the six-yard box.

Near Post
Usually the area in front of the near post rather than the post itself. Offside rule plays a big part as to how far out the Near Post area will be.

Re-starts
Another term used to describe Set Plays.

Screen Player
An attacking player or players who stand in position to affect the ability of the goalkeeper to see the ball.

Set Pieces
Another term used to describe Set Plays.

Thirds of the Field
The soccer field is divided by the rules into two halves, but in coaching terms the three equal thirds of the field are used to describe tactical considerations

Wall Man
A member of a human wall set up by the defending team to make it difficult to get a shot at goal on a Free Kick near the penalty box.

Zona Rosa (or the Red Zone)
A small area of approximately one-yard radius 3 to 4 yards off the goal line and 2 to 3 yards inside the line of the near post that is difficult to defend and particularly productive at attacking corner kicks.

A Game of Opinions!
Tell Us What You Think!

As the old coach would say: "There are many ways up Everest!" And so there are. Some are better than others! Some are still uncharted!

One of the great aspects of soccer is that everyone develops opinions about the game.

In this book, we have used our experiences to try to be as "on-the-ball" as possible. But don't be afraid to question us. Or blatantly disagree!

A few years ago, I read a book on Set Plays and could have used a red pen on nearly every page. In my opinion, 30% was incorrect or misleading and would've affected coaches and their teams negatively if they followed the suggestions.

I can guarantee that we are better than 90% right, but I doubt if we are 100%...maybe 99%!

Call, fax or email if there is something you don't agree with or is not clear. We want and respect your opinions and will review and modify the book with each print.

Telephone:	1-800-762-2378
Fax:	1-604-921-8964
Email:	info@worldofsoccer.com

The Last Word

The Principles of Set Plays is the guideline for success.

As coach, you must evaluate the abilities and disabilities of your players in the game and in practice.

Set up fun challenges and games to test the abilities of your players.

Who strikes and flights the best Corners?

Who has the ability and timing to flick-on the ball from a Free Kick or Corner?

It's pretty obvious that if the first ball in on a Corner Kick is poor, we have wasted a lot of time and energy in putting our best players into their most effective scoring positions.

Who is your bravest "Bullet Man?"

Who are the best five players for a Penalty Shootout?

Are they good in practice? More importantly: Can they stand up to the pressure of competition?

Spend 25% or more of your team practice time on Set Plays.

If you want that 10-goal difference in a season of 20 or more games, the difference that I guaranteed at the beginning of this book, you must make sure to give yourself the best chance of scoring and preventing goals.

Remember, too…your players are not robots. They will make mistakes. Some will be particularly good in certain roles on Set Plays. Some may appear to be good in certain situations, but can't handle the responsibility. You have to make the decisions of who does what and then manage the situation of potentially bruised egos, while at the same time trying to maintain the all-round team and individual confidences.

So finally here comes the small print.

To guarantee the 10-goal difference a season, you must apply the teachings of this book. If the coaches you go against also have this book, it nullifies the guarantee! If the coaches you compete against have this book and they've applied the principles and methodology and you haven't, LOOK OUT! The 10-goal difference is theirs!

Just joking! Good luck and good coaching!

Tony Waiters

The World of Soccer Coaching Series

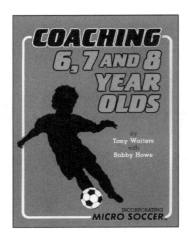

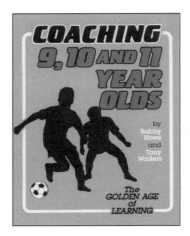

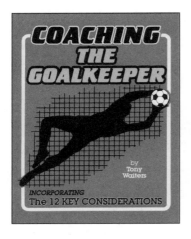

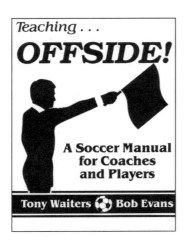

Fun Books for Younger Players

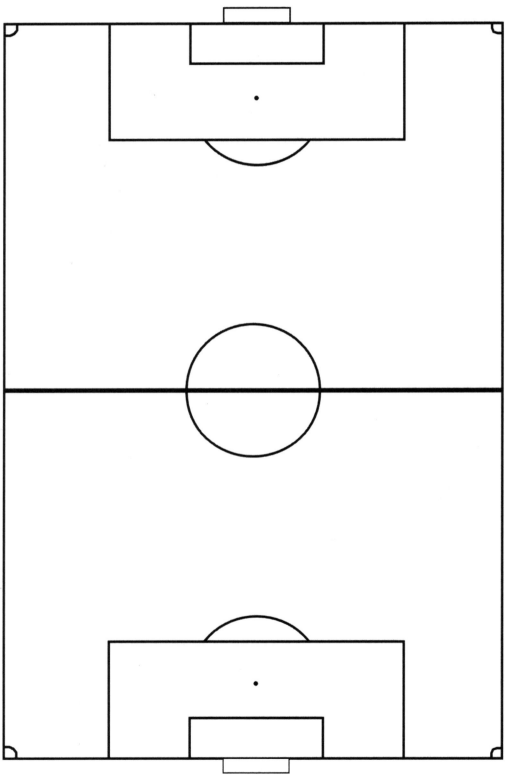

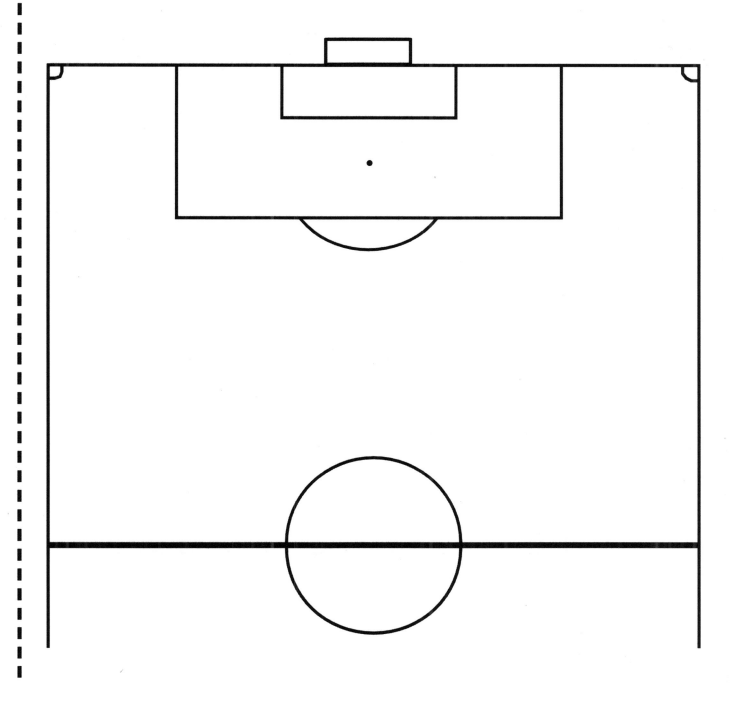

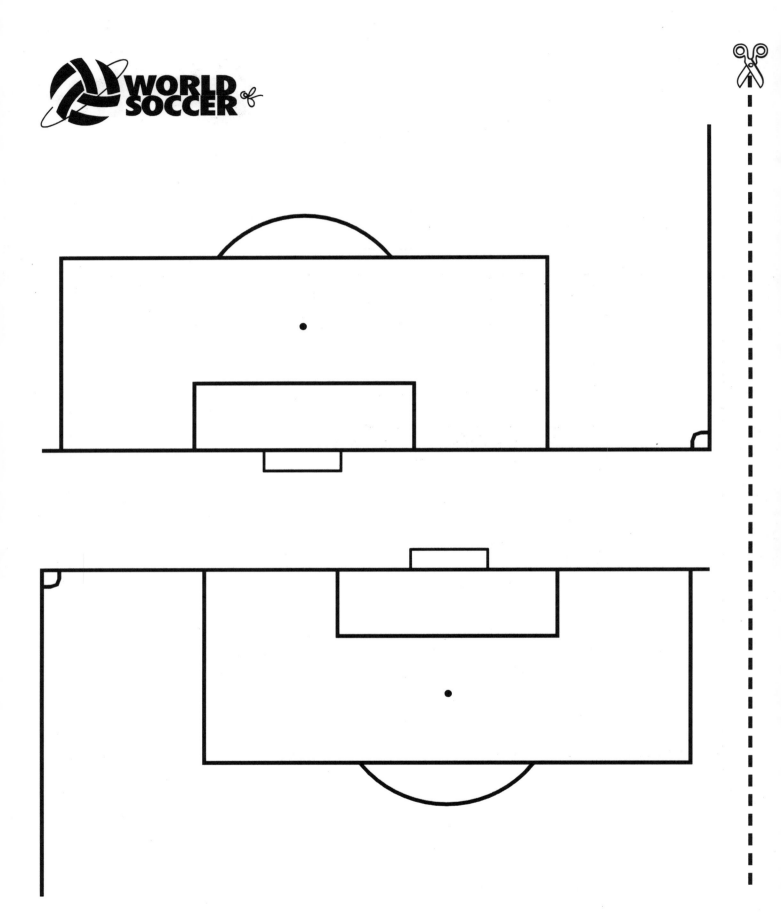